Fathers&Sons

"The most common 'male illness' today is 'Too little father in the years from birth to fifteen.' The Schreur men offer every man abundant 'windows' on father and son opportunities for satisfying the deep hungers of boys for father time."

DONALD M. JOY,
Professor of Human Development & Family Studies,
Asbury Seminary

"This book is a marvelous resource, awakening fathers to their role as men in the burgeoning men's movement and in their calling as dads."

JACK W. HAYFORD, Senior Pastor, The Church on the Way

Fathers & Sons

Jack & Jerry Schreur

VICTOR BOOKS

A DIVISION OF SCRIPTURE PRESS PUBLICATIONS INC.
USA CANADA ENGLAND

Scripture quotations are from the *Holy Bible, New International Version®*.
Copyright © 1973, 1978, 1984 by International Bible Society.
Used by permission of Zondervan Publishing House.
All rights reserved.

Copy Editors: Rachel Derowitsch and Greg Clouse
Cover Designer: Scott Rattray
Cover Photo: Bill Bilsley

ISBN: 1-56476-432-X

1   2   3   4   5   6   7   8   9   10   Printing/Year   99   98   97   96   95

For my dad, who loved me unconditionally,
and my sons, Jack and Jon,
who I love beyond measure and
who have become lifelong friends.

Jerry Schreur

For my father, who is my best friend,
his father, who taught him well,
and especially for my son Jonathon,
whom I have tried to love with
both patience and abandon.

Jack Schreur

Contents

Acknowledgments

Dad and I would like to thank all of the fathers and sons who shared their stories with us, and in doing so shared their lives with everyone who reads this book. Thanks for your openness, your unguarded speech, and your joyful spirits. We are all the richer for your gift to us.

We would also like to thank Greg Clouse at Victor Books for his patience, encouragement, and support of this project. After working with Greg on two books, we don't consider him merely an editor, he has become a friend.

To my family who watched and waited for their father to return to normal, noses pressing against the glass door of my office, as this book neared completion. Thanks Leslie, Erin, Jonathon, and Kendall, for your patience, your love, your support, and your smiles. I love you all very much!

And finally to my father, you are the inspiration and the model for this book. Thanks for working with me, for sharing your life with me, for being my friend. I love you, Dad.

Chapter One
An Enduring Love

It was 1973. I was nine years old, sitting with my brother and my father in the "friendly confines" of Wrigley Field. We were, of course, watching the Chicago Cubs play, and as any Cubs fan would guess, we were watching them lose. Baseball plays a special role in my life: my father was at one time a good player, and some of my earliest memories are of the two of us playing catch, and of him and my brother and me going to Cubs games. I spent almost five years in the Chicago area when I was in grade school, and my father was the pastor of a small church. We didn't have much money, but somehow we managed to make it to five or six Cubs games a year. Those were great occasions for a young, left-handed, wannabe first baseman.

On this day most of the crowd had left Wrigley Field early to try to beat the traffic. The Cubs had played an uninspired game, trailing the whole way. I had been begging my father since the seventh-inning stretch to leave, but his reply had been the same each time: "Hold on, boy. The game's not over yet. Just hold your horses." I watched the other people leave, and then a miracle of sorts occurred. With two outs in the ninth inning, the opposing pitcher walked a Cubs batter. The next batter slapped a bloop single to left, which brought Billy Williams to the plate, the star of the Cubs during those years. Two on, two out, the Cubs down by two. He represented the winning run. My brother and I leaped to our feet as he lined the first pitched past us down the third base line — just foul. We groaned as we sat back down. The next pitch was high and outside for a ball. Williams hit the next pitch foul, again past third base. Two strikes and two outs. It didn't look good for the Cubs. Ahead in the count, the pitcher threw a sweeping curve that hung in the strike zone a split second too long, and Williams crushed the ball into the centerfield bleachers. The game was over and the Cubs had won! My dad grabbed me and my brother and we jumped up and down. "Aren't you glad we waited, Jack? Aren't you glad we stayed?"

On the way home Dad mused to himself, just loud enough for me to hear, "I wonder how all those people who left early felt listening to the game on their car radios, hearing Jack Brickhouse call Billy Williams' home run. I wonder how they felt?"

I knew how I felt. I felt my dad was probably the smartest man in the whole world, and I knew I was lucky to have him for my dad. A dad who seemed to know that Billy Williams would step to the plate and hit the winning home run. A dad who said, "What's your hurry, boy?" hugged me close, and let me know that he loved me too much to let me leave early and miss the best part.

When I was thirteen years old, he brought home a little motorcycle one day. It was a gift from a friend whose children were too old for the bike — and besides, it didn't run. "If you want to fix it, you can have it." And so my dad took it and fixed it and then gave it to my brother and me to ride in the woods. By this time we had moved to Michigan, where my father was the director of a Christian camp. We were surrounded by acres of woods and trails, and I got to know every one of them on that little Honda 90. Every once in a while we would ride the bike too hard, or it would just quit working. We'd walk it home and Dad would look at it, seemingly taking it apart randomly and talking all the while to my brother and me. "Look at that, boys," pointing to a mysterious, greasy engine part. "I bet that's the trouble. I would bet you that if we do this. . . ." His voice would trail off, and he would put the bike back together, always with a part or two left over. My brother, who worried about leftover parts, would ask, "Where was this bolt supposed to go, Dad?" My dad always said the same thing: "Don't worry about it. Let's see if she'll run." I'd give it a kick, it would start, and once again I would know that my father was someone special.

Times change and so do little boys' ideas about their fathers. In time I no longer believed that my father had all the answers. As a matter of fact, a time came when I thought I had all the answers and that he was completely wrong. I was sixteen when I gathered my courage, looked him in the eye, and said, "Dad, I don't believe in God anymore. I've been thinking about it a lot, and it just doesn't make sense to me. So I don't think that I'll be going to church with you anymore." I paused and waited for the stern answer, or a lecture, or anger, or anything. After all, my father was a professor at a Bible college and an ordained minister. His faith was everything to him. I knew a storm would have to come. But he just looked at me and shook his head a little. "OK, Jack, fine." Emboldened by his acceptance, I decided to push a little further. "By the way, Dad, I don't think I'm going to pray before I eat anymore. Since I don't believe in God, I don't really think it makes sense to pray to Him. So I probably won't be having dinner much with the family anymore." Another slight shake of the head. As I turned to walk out the door, he said, "By the way, Jack, where were you planning on living?" I turned around quickly. "What do you mean? I'm going to live here." He shook his head slowly and uttered the immortal words so many fathers over so many genera-tions have said: "If you want to live in my house, drink my milk, eat my food, and sleep under my roof, you are going to play by my rules. But, hey, it's up to you. If you've got another place to go, that's up to you." I had seventy-nine cents in my pocket and thirty-four dollars in the bank. I had no place to go and really didn't want to leave, even if I could. I was in church that Sunday.

Adolescence is not always an easy time, and my teen years were probably less easy than most people's. But my father never gave up on me. When I was rude to him or treated him badly, he never quit loving me; and somehow through that difficult time in my life I loved my father more deeply than I ever had as a child. I no longer thought of him as perfect. Instead, I became aware of a

man who lived what he said he believed and did what he said he
would do. As a teenager I fought with my father. We argued about
music, about what kind of person I was, about girls, and about
church. But he never lied to me and never went back on his word.
He never made me feel stupid. He listened to my ideas and then
discussed them with me. He treated me like a human being.

My dad has been an active part of my life for longer than I can
remember. He took me on my first motorcycle ride when I was
twelve months old. I'm told I sat on the gas tank between his legs
as we went to visit my grandparents. He has been a part of my life
ever since, but somewhere in those difficult years between fourteen
and twenty my father became something more meaningful to me.
He became my best friend. I'm on the other side of thirty now,
and the mythical image I had of my father when I was a child has
been replaced by an honest appraisal of the all-too-human, fifty-
three-year-old man. But one thing hasn't changed. My father is
still my best friend. We travel together, speak together, work
together, write together, argue together, and get mad together.
Through it all we have built a deep and abiding friendship that has
stood the test of time and the vagaries of life. We have built a
friendship to last a lifetime.

My friend Will's story is very different from mine. As Will tells it,
"The only thing I ever got from my father was the back of his
hand. I can't ever remember my father telling me that he loved me
or that I was important to him. When I was sixteen years old, he
walked out of my life, and the only time I've seen him since is in
court, trying to get him to pay my mom the child support he
owes." Will is now twenty-three, married, and the father of an
eighteen-month-old boy. When I talked to him about this book, he
looked at me for a long moment and then began to cry. "Jack,
write something that will tell me how to avoid being the kind of
dad my dad was. You have a great dad, and you guys are really
fun together. But so many of us haven't had that kind of relationship. We just don't know how to build a strong relationship with
our sons."

Fathers and Sons is about building a friendship that will last a
lifetime. It is not just for fathers who have had terrific modeling

from their own dads. It is not just for fathers who have strong, healthy marriages. This book is for every father who wants to grow closer to his son. The fathering strengths we have discovered apply to single fathers, African-American fathers, Anglo fathers — fathers of every age and race. Any father who reads these pages will walk away inspired by the stories of dads and sons who are forging real friendships. Any dad who works his way through this book will walk away knowing exactly what he has to do and how to do it. But don't take that to mean that there are ten magical steps or some secrets you haven't been let in on yet. We don't pretend to have discovered some long-hidden truth or stumbled upon a fool-proof way to father. This book is about the process of making our boys men, staying close to them, and building a friendship with them during that process.

Building a strong relationship with your son takes effort, although it is enjoyable effort. It requires intentionality. That means we need to set a goal of having strong friendships with our sons, and we have to make sure that our actions, words, and attitude will get us to our goal. A lifetime friendship with our sons doesn't just happen. We have to build into our lives the fathering strengths that have carried other fathers and sons through difficult times. We need to be proactive, constantly seeking ways to build the habits that will strengthen our relationships.

What you won't find here are a lot of negative examples. We won't spend our time talking about what is wrong with fathers today and how little time they spend with their sons and so on. Instead, in these pages you will meet many different fathers and sons. And we mean *meet* them. These are real people with real jobs, real lives, real struggles, and real triumphs. Most chapters begin with a brief biography of the families featured in that chapter. No names have been changed; everyone of these people have agreed to share their stories in the hope that their lives will inspire you.

All of these fathers have developed a positive relationship with their sons. They have done that in different ways, using their unique gifts and personalities. These are not perfect relationships. Many of them have been tested by the refiner's fire of difficult times and hardships. Some of them are young fathers; some of them are grandfathers. Some of them are materially well off; some struggle to pay the bills. Some are married; some are single. Some of them had great fathers; some of them didn't. But the one thing these different people share is a commitment to their sons and to becoming the best fathers they can be.

In this book you also will come to know me; my son, Jonathon; my brother, Jon; my father (who is the coauthor of this book); and my grandfather. Our relationships have had their difficulties and their heartaches, but through it all these four generations of men and boys have been fast friends. And the respect and love we have engendered is remarkable. Through our lives and the stories of other real-life fathers, you will see how we have built our friendships. And in these stories you will find a blueprint that will enable you to shape your friendship with your son.

Through our research on strong families and on strong father-son relationships, Dad and I have discovered some relationship qualities that enable fathers and sons to build a friendship for a lifetime. We call these fathering strengths. There are eleven of these qualities, and if you are looking for a secret to a successful father-son relationship, these qualities are your answer. But they are not a secret. Most of the fathering strengths are common sense, although they are not common. They do not require special abilities or schooling. You don't need a lot of money to build these qualities into your life. What you need is dedication and hard work.

The eleven relationship qualities are:

Time Together	Opportunities for quality experiences and mutual satisfaction.
Commitment	Helping each other be all we can be.
Play and Laughter	Taking a lighthearted look at life. Being alert to and spontaneously responding to opportunities to enjoy life.
Affirmation and Appreciation	Recognizing qualities in each other and expressing appreciation for those qualities.

Adaptability	Changing to meet the demands of the environment and relationship.
Positive Communication	Transferring of information, both verbally and nonverbally, that builds others up and never tears them down.
Trust and Respect	Earning the confidence and regard of our sons and giving them our esteem and honor.
Conflict Resolution	The ability to deal with differences, resolve conflict, and cope with crisis.
Forgiveness	Canceling debts incurred and starting fresh every day.
Spiritual Wellness	A sense of personal completeness and peace with God, knowing that we are loved, accepted, and forgiven by Him.
Cohesion	Emotional closeness resulting in sharing yourself with one another.

There is no guarantee that you and your son will be able to forge a lifetime friendship. Ultimately, both of you have to choose to do that. You have to agree to share your lives and to love each other. But any father, regardless of his son's age, can begin to put these principles into practice in his relationship with his son. And if you do that, good things will happen. If you are fortunate enough to be reading this book as a new father, these qualities need to be a part of your life as your son grows into this world, with all of its pitfalls and problems. You are in a unique position to commit yourself to doing it right. Your entire relationship is before you. You can frame that relationship, its tenor and tone, right now and begin the long road of fathering a son and growing into a lifelong friendship.

Many of you reading this book have had it handed to you by your wife or by a friend. Maybe your children are already in junior high or high school, and you are wondering if it is too late to begin building these qualities into your life. The answer is that there is no time like the present, and time's-a-wastin'! If your son is a teenager, this is a terrific time to begin to work on the fathering strengths. Perhaps at no other time in his life will your son need you more than he does right now as he builds his identity and makes his way through adolescence. You will have to be patient and move at his pace and be aware of his needs, but you can do it.

Some of you looking at this book have grown sons. They have left the house and are starting families of their own. Maybe you feel like you have blown it, that you have already missed the opportunity to develop a lifelong friendship with your children. And reading these opening pages has only made you despair for the missed opportunities and the lost years. Our message to you is one of hope. Don't give up. Even at this late stage in the game, it is possible to put these qualities to work in your life and to begin to rebuild a relationship with your son. Don't let another day go by before you start down the road to healing with your son.

Ultimately, this book is for fathers of all ages who want to share their lives with their sons. It is for fathers who realize or are beginning to realize that building a business or a career and accumulating things don't add up to much in the long run. Not when those things are compared with a significant and vital relationship with our sons. This book is for fathers who want to pass on their values to their sons, who want to be a vital part in their lives, and who want an enduring friendship that will bring them joy and happiness all their lives.

Running through this book is another theme. We believe that fathering a son, nurturing him, and building him into a man is a spiritual journey. Fathering is a calling of God, and we cannot do it without Him. We know, from the proving ground of real life, that fathering can be a trying, difficult task. But we also know that God strengthens us along the way and calls us to Him through our sons. Finally, we believe that our greatest responsibility as fathers is to live lives that will draw our sons closer to God, and that ultimately what matters is that our boys become followers of Jesus.

We wrote *Fathers and Sons* because our relationship is one of the most important things in our lives. I talk to my father every day on the phone. Sometimes we talk about work, sometimes I ask advice, sometimes he asks for advice. Sometimes we talk football, sometimes we talk about God, sometimes we talk about my brother. (Jon doesn't know this.) But if I don't talk to my dad on a given day I feel like I have missed out, because he is my best male friend, and I choose to share my joys and sorrows with him.

Why is it important to build a relationship like this with your sons? Because as fathers we have enormous importance in their lives. They look to us for acceptance, for love and, most of all, for an idea of what it means to be a man. And we need to be there for them. But fathering isn't all work and no play. Through this friendship with your son you will have fun, you will find joy, and you will experience God's love and His pleasure in your relationship. It is a double win. If you commit yourself to building a strong relationship with your son, he wins because he has a consistent friend, mentor, and role model. You win by passing along your values, watching your son grow into a man, and enjoying life with him.

So take a stand today. Commit yourself to building a strong friendship with your son. Read on to the end of the book, and build the fathering strengths into your life. Thousands of men across America will do that this year, and they will not be sorry that they took the time to build an enduring relationship with their sons.

Fathers and Sons Commitments

	Yes	No	Not Sure
1. I am committed to creating an environment of love and acceptance for my son.	—	—	—
2. I am committed to being creatively involved in my son's life.	—	—	—
3. I commit myself to coming to grips with my past in order to become a better father.	—	—	—

Chapter Two

To Every Generation

Gerry and Dan Borreson couldn't have chosen more different ways to earn a living. Gerry is a retired factory worker; his son Dan is a respected surgeon. What they share is a dedication to hard work done well, and a twinkle in their eyes that lights especially when they are talking about each other and their friendship.

My father grew up on a farm. His father was a celery farmer in the little town of Hudsonville, Michigan. Growing up on the farm and working with my grandfather had a profound impact on my dad. And my brother and I could never hear enough about it. As a result, Dad often would repeat his favorite stories, and one such story is about a boring summer afternoon, a lawn mower, and—as is always the case with my dad—leftover parts.

My ten-year-old dad was fascinated by mechanical things. Car engines, tractor engines, even the push lawn mower. One boring summer day his fascination could no longer wait. He was dying to see what made a lawn mower cut grass and what it looked like from the inside out. The only way to learn that, of course, was to take it apart. So he pushed my grandpa's lawn mower behind the barn, sat down in the dirt with a couple of wrenches and a screwdriver, and began to explore the lawn mower. Two and a half hours later, every nut and bolt was apart. The lawn mower

21

had been well examined. There was, however, one small problem: my dad had no idea how to put the thing back together. Every time he tried, a multitude of parts was left over, and the mower refused to work. After trying to hide the mower from my grandpa for nearly the entire day, he finally summoned his courage and confessed to his father that he had taken the mower apart to see what made it work but that he was unable to get it back together.

My grandfather responded in an interesting way. Instead of yelling at my dad for possibly ruining a needed and expensive piece of equipment, he sat down with him and tried to put the mower together with him. But even together, Dad and Grandpa were unable to get it to work again — ever. (It is the curse of our family always to have leftover parts.) My dad can't remember exactly what his father said to him, but he remembers how he felt as he sat in the grass with his father trying to put the mower back together.

He tells it this way: "I can't really explain what happened that day, but I knew that my dad loved me and that he accepted me. We were a poor family. Our farm was small, a subsistence living. The mower was expensive for us. But my dad actually seemed glad that I had shown an interest in mechanical stuff and that I wanted to know how everything worked. After that he allowed me to work on the other farm machinery, and eventually I became a good mechanic, able to fix anything. I point to that experience, where I could have been shot down by my dad for wrecking the mower, as an important event in my life. Because in spite of the fact that I couldn't put it together again, my dad made me feel good about my interest in mechanics, and he made me feel special because of it. I remember one thing he said to me that day, 'Well, boy, not everybody could have done as thorough a job taking this mower apart. You really needed to know, didn't you?' I know those words don't sound like much, but to a scared ten-year-old boy they communicated volumes."

When I asked my father what he learned from his father about being a dad, he mentioned two things. The first is that my grandpa always let my dad know that he was loved and accepted. Now, my father's boyhood was during the forties and early fifties, and fathers then didn't speak words of love or show affection as easily as they do today. But somehow my grandpa got the message through to my dad that he was special and that he was a loved and valuable person — in spite of my dad's difficult and serious troubles as a teenager.

The second thing my father mentions when he talks about Grandpa is that he taught my father that life is meant to be lived and enjoyed. Life is not just a struggle; in the struggle there is joy, fun, and friendship. My grandpa never had much. Dad was very poor growing up. In spite of that, my dad never felt like they were poor. It was only in hindsight, looking back over his childhood, that Dad realizes how poor they were. Grandpa always focused on what they could do instead of what they couldn't. If they couldn't afford to go out to eat, so what? They could afford to stop for a Coke. They could afford to hunt and fish together, activities that provided both food for a family of nine and a father and oldest son lots of time together.

These two lessons are important because my father taught them to me, and I want to teach them to my son. Although my grandfather didn't know it, he was beginning a tradition that has been handed down now to the fourth generation, a tradition of love and acceptance and an enjoyment of life. What you and I do as fathers is profoundly affected by what our fathers did. And their fathering was profoundly affected by what their fathers did. Fathering is an intergenerational issue. We are, at least in part, what our fathers have made us, and we need to realize that as we dedicate ourselves to becoming the best fathers we can be for our sons.

The Scriptures talk about the sins of the fathers being passed on to the fourth generation (Numbers 14:18). And many of us can point to negative traits in our character that seem to be intergenerational. There is another aspect to that though. Just as the sins of the fathers are passed on, so too are the positive characteristics. Instead of passing on sins we can pass on strengths. Too many times we dwell on the negative things our fathers have taught us, and we don't realize the positive things we have gained from them.

I was talking with a forty-five-year-old man some time ago. He remarked that his entire life he had been angry with his father for

not spending more time with him, for not giving him more affection and outward expressions of love. This man blamed his father
for his troubles and had been in therapy for a long time. When his
father called with the news that he had cancer, this man went
home to spend time with his dad. In doing so he realized something he hadn't thought of before. As he watched his father, he
suddenly understood that his dad had taught him many things
that had helped him grow into an adult. He noticed especially the
way his father treated his mother with kindness, gentleness, and
love. This forty-five-year-old man realized that his own marriage,
the source of so much strength and comfort in his life, had been
modeled on his parents', and that the way he treated his wife was
much like the way his father treated his mother. And this man
thanked his father for the first time in twenty years.

We can choose to look at our fathers and see the good things
that they have passed on to us. We can sift through our childhood
and find the things they have taught us that are worth passing
down to our own sons. Our heritage can become a source of joy
and strength instead of a source of shame. It is useless to pretend
that our fathering is not influenced by the way we were fathered.
Whether we realize it or not, it is probably the most powerful
influence of our fathering styles. For some of us that is good news;
for others it is not.

I spent twenty minutes today throwing my son around the living
room. Before you call a child protection agency, you must understand that he asked for it. He really did. Jonathon literally asked
me to throw him around the room. In fact, he nearly begged me
for it. "Dad, can we roughhouse now?" he asked with a slight
whine to his voice. In my family, roughhousing has a long and
storied tradition. My father wrestled with me, playing tough, roll-
ing around with me, tossing me gently about, and I loved it. It was
natural for me to do the same thing with my son. I never had to
think about it. Playing like that with Jonathon is instinctive; because my father had done it, I thought everybody did it. And I bet
that some day my son will do the same thing with his son. This
Schreur tradition is a source of joy and strengthens our
relationships.

But what if the tradition in your family isn't roughhousing, but abuse? Or it is coldness, or a lack of acceptance, or some other negative, intergenerational trait? Does that mean you are destined to repeat the mistakes of your father? Is it impossible for you to break out of that cycle and start new with your son? Some of us have not had good role modeling from our fathers; they haven't had it from their fathers, and so on. Often we feel that we are almost powerless to stop the cycle of dysfunction and pain. We wonder how we can ever be good fathers when we have no model to follow.

The good news is that this book is full of stories of fathers who had to break out of destructive intergenerational cycles. In their stories you will find the role model you lacked growing up. Hearing how they have broken free will give you both the courage and the road map to enable you to start new, positive, intergenerational traditions. You have a unique opportunity to shape the father-son relationships in your family for generations to come. You can instill the qualities in your sons that you know they need, and some of those values will be passed to your grandkids and to your great-grandkids. What you do right will have an impact far beyond your lifetime.

We can take the good things we learned from our fathers and translate them to our sons. We can begin passing down new characteristics and traditions that begin with us but don't end with us. It is possible to stop the cycle of destructive relationship qualities. It is possible to build the fathering strengths into your life even if your father was not the man he should have been. While you are building the fathering strengths into your life, you are also helping build them into your grandson's life and beyond that. What an amazing opportunity we have as fathers to influence future generations. What an awesome responsibility.

Gerry and Dan Borreson will tell you that they are simply living out scripts already prepared for them. Gerry's dad was a terrific father. Gerry has been a great father, and now Dan's desire is to be worthy of the fathering tradition in his family. Gerry's father had a sixth-grade education. Gerry is a World War II vet and retired factory worker who never finished high school. Dan is a successful surgeon. But these three Borreson men have forged an intergenerational tradition of loving, involved fathering. Dan relates: "We're so much alike, my dad and I, that my wife, Dawn, points out that we walk the same and we have a lot of the same expressions and gestures. Dawn starts laughing and says, 'You're just like your dad.' And that's a good thing. I didn't know my grandfather very well, but from what I know of him, my dad is a lot like he was."

Gerry laughs, "It may be a gene — who knows? I learned how to deal with people from my dad. I have only fond memories of my father, nothing bad at all. As a matter of fact, after my dad died I had more dreams about him being alive than I ever did of my mother. He was a very loving person. There was a closeness there. Maybe because we worked at the same place. If he had a few minutes he would come over and visit with me."

As we talked with Dan and Gerry, it was apparent they realize they are a part of something far bigger than themselves. They are merely the latest in a line of good fathers, and they both feel a responsibility to keep that going. In Dan's words, "I recognize the relationship chain we have going. I don't want to break that chain." Gerry took the good things he learned from his father about spending time with his son and followed through. "My dad was always there for me," Dan adds. "We knew he was always coming home to us, that he would do what he said he would do. He came to my games in high school. He was there."

Although their education levels differ and their occupations are worlds apart, Dan points to his father as inspiration even in his practice as a surgeon. "I view my father as a craftsman. He was the kind of guy who went in and did eight hours and put in his best for the time he was at work. He was proud of his work. It's something I learned from him."

Gerry and Dan aren't perfect parents. They haven't done everything right; they have made mistakes. But they have taken the good things handed down to them and have built on that legacy. Dan ends his thoughts on his dad with these powerful words: "What my dad has given to me, to all of us kids, and to the grandkids is far more valuable than any material thing he can give us. My dad has given us love and respect."

To ignore the way we were fathered is impossible. Like Gerry and Dan, we need to begin to understand that how we were raised is affecting the way we parent. Getting a handle on the way we are fathering our sons, or the way we want to father our sons, means that we must at least begin to come to terms with the way we were fathered. That involves asking at least two questions and doing a key thing:

1. *What intergenerational strengths did my father pass down to me?*

2. *What intergenerational dysfunction and pain did my father hand to me?*

3. *Purpose to make peace with your father.*

What Our Fathers Did Right

The first question is a positive one that is unasked and underappreciated by too many men. We spend a great deal of time in the nineties examining our "father wound," and many of us can pinpoint exactly what our fathers did wrong in raising us. The question we fail to ask and the examination we fail to make involves what our fathers did right with us. Most of our fathers did their best. Few of them were truly evil men. Even those of us who have had lousy fathering role models had dads who did their best, even if their best was sabotaged by anger, alcohol, irresponsibility, or something else. Most of us have had some fathering strengths passed down to us. And we need to take advantage of the positive intergenerational modeling and pass those strengths down to our sons.

Doug is forty-three years old and just coming to terms with the death of his alcoholic father two years ago. Doug's memories of his dad are not positive. He remembers the shame of living with an alcoholic. He is still dealing with issues of codependency, anger, and self-esteem that are rooted in his complex relationship with his father. It is easy for Doug to point out what was wrong with his dad. It is easy for Doug to tell what he wants to do differently with his teenage boys. But it is much more difficult for Doug to pinpoint the fathering strengths that his father passed down. After all, he has spent half a lifetime blaming his dad for almost every bad thing that happened to him. But recently Doug has been making a more honest appraisal of his father. He realizes that although his father was not the man he should have been, he was not the devil Doug and his therapy had been making him out to be.

"I can remember some terrific times with my dad," Doug says. "They came during my junior high years when my father was sober for almost three years. He taught me how to build stuff. My dad was a construction worker, and he could always work with wood. When I was about twelve years old he invited me out into his workshop for the first time. Well, I had been there before, but only to tell him that dinner was ready, or that I needed him to take me somewhere, or to help him sweep up. This time he invited me in to work with him. I'll never forget it. We made, over the course of almost three weeks, an intricate birdhouse. Then he let me help him paint it. Over that time he talked to me, and I kind of got to know him. He let me know what his father had been like. We talked about him growing up, and we kept building stuff. It was really great. I found out that his father had been a heavy drinker, but that he had learned how to work with wood from him. And now some thirty years later I'm teaching the same things to my sons. They're having a great time learning, and I'm getting a tremendous amount of satisfaction out of teaching them. Last night, I actually audibly thanked my dad for those times. They have become a source of joy in my life now."

Doug is learning to look for the good in his relationship with his father and build that good into his relationship with his sons. All of us need to do that. We need to look in our background, identify the things our fathers did right, and then emulate them. That is how intergenerational strengths and a tradition of strong fathering is built.

To realize the strengths your dad passed down to you, you might need to spend some time with your father if he is still living and if your relationship is amicable. Ask what he thought about raising you. Ask him about societal attitudes toward fathers in his day. Try to get a clearer picture of him, his motives, and his reasons. Then it will be easier to pass on his strengths to your son.

Do yourself a favor in the next few minutes. Put this book down and take some time to think about the good things that you have learned from your father. Ask your wife or your brothers or sisters for input. Then write down the things you would like to emulate about that relationship. But don't stop there. If your father is still alive, call him and let him know that you appreciated his efforts in fathering you and that you intend to pass along those things to your son. I guarantee you that it will make his day.

Where Our Fathers Fell Short

The second thing we need to do to come to grips with the inter-generational aspects of fathering is to look at the way we were fathered and determine the negative things we have learned from our fathers. We need not dwell on or castigate our fathers for them. But it is important to see what we don't want to repeat so we can stop the cycle of poor fathering that infects many families.

This may be difficult for many of us to do. It seems disloyal to go back twenty or thirty years and disapprove of what our fathers did. It seems unfair to hold them accountable to the parenting standards of today. Realize, though, that we aren't doing this to confront our fathers or excise the demons that haunt us. We aren't trying to bring them down or knock them off their pedestals. We simply want to learn what we don't want to repeat.

I have a difficult time with this. My dad and I are very close, and subjecting our positive relationship to negative scrutiny seems counterproductive. But it isn't. As Dad said not long ago, "Jack, I wasn't the perfect dad. If I had to do it all over again I would have been different. I would have been less controlling, more open, and not as cold when you guys were younger. Don't put me up on a pedestal. I'm bound to fall off." Dad is right. Although he was a remarkable father, he wasn't perfect. He's not a reflective man, and his eldest son is. That caused conflict between us, and only by being honest about that can I hope to not repeat his mistakes.

My dad was more athletic than I was, and sometimes his attempts to teach me sports were met with less than success. I remember when I joined Little League and wanted to be a first baseman. My dad was an excellent pitcher in his youth. I had a major problem for a first baseman — I was afraid of the ball. When it was thrown to me I would close my eyes and stick my glove out and hope that the ball would miraculously end up there. This is not a good quality in a boy with aspirations to be a first baseman, because people are constantly throwing balls at you and it is your job to catch them.

My dad took me into the backyard, determined to cure me of my fear of the baseball. He explained to me that the best chance I had of getting hit with a baseball came when my eyes were closed, and the best chance I had of avoiding that calamity was by keeping my eyes open and on the ball. I nodded vigorously and we went to work. He started by throwing me slow, easy balls to build my confidence, and it seemed to work. Gradually, he increased the velocity and started throwing at my body. I was beginning to feel confident when he threw a hard one right at my face. Instinctively, I threw my glove up and closed my eyes. The ball whistled past my glove and thunked me just below the right eye. I fell to the ground, stunned and surprised, but mostly in pain. My father dropped his glove, ran over to me, picked me up, and carried me into our house. Luckily, nothing was broken or even seriously hurt. But I had a black eye, and I remember lying there with the ice pack covering most of my face and Father, realizing I was going to be OK, saying, "Jackson, boy, that is why you must not close your eyes." Truth, perhaps, but hardly what a boy in my condition needed to hear.

Last month I was in the backyard throwing a baseball to my son who, lo and behold, has the same problem that afflicted me. He closes his eyes when the ball gets close. (Talk about intergenerational issues!) I heard myself utter the same lecture that my father had given me about catching a baseball with my eyes closed. But looking back upon my experience, I decided the best thing I could do for Jonathon was to get a softer ball before I tempted fate by throwing at his face. So I did. But then I attempted to teach him the same way my father taught me, and lo and behold, I hit him right on the nose. Down he went. It was a familiar sight.

I relate that story because in a simple way it illustrates how the same problems can haunt our fathering from generation to generation. Most of those problems are far more serious than a game of catch, but they work the same way. We end up making the same mistakes our fathers made with us if we don't scrutinize the way we were fathered and make a conscious effort not to do the same things. This is especially important for dads who had a difficult relationship with their fathers. Take a hard look at what intergenerational struggles are manifested in your fathering. Ask your wife or a close friend for input. Write down the things your father did that you believe damaged your relationship, and then carefully and honestly examine your fathering patterns. Only by doing this can we hope to break through cycles of dysfunction.

Making Peace with Our Fathers

Last, it is important to make peace with your father. If your relationship with your father is broken or damaged, we encourage you to do what you can to be reconciled with him. That process is beyond the scope of this book, but we believe strongly that making peace with your father is an important step in becoming the father God wants you to be. It may require some counseling, some prayer, or just some old-fashioned talking, but it is a step you must take. An important resource in making peace with your father is a book by Gordon Dalbey entitled *Father and Son: The Wound, the Healing, the Call to Manhood.* And while it is not our purpose to spend a great deal of time on this subject, we cannot stress enough how big a part forgiveness must play in this process. It is time to start forgiving your father for his shortcomings and getting on with your fathering. Don't drag the bitterness and difficulty into yet another generation. Make this time in your life the place where you stand as a man before God, forgiving your father and purposing to build a strong tradition of fathering for your sons.

Fathering is a tough job that can be made tougher if we haven't had a role model in our own fathers. But it is not hopeless or impossible. We can break the cycle of negative fathering relationships. We can make a difference in the lives of our sons. We can become the fathers God wants us to be. But we have to deal with our own fathers first, taking from them the strengths that impacted our lives, letting go of the negatives that might have plagued our family for generations, and forgiving our fathers.

Intergenerational Checklist

	Yes	No
1. I can readily think of strengths (positive characteristics) my father has passed on to me.	___	___
2. I find it easy to focus on the positive characteristics of my father.	___	___
3. I am still struggling with negative experiences with my father.	___	___
4. I am grateful for my father's influence on my life.	___	___
5. I have told my father how much he means to me.	___	___
6. I am trying to change my focus from the negative characteristics of my father to his positive qualities.	___	___
7. I need outside help to deal with issues related to my father, such as healing and forgiveness.	___	___
8. I have forgiven my father for past wrongs and mistakes.	___	___

9. I regularly express to my father my
   appreciation for him.   ___ ___

10. I am committed to being the best father I can
    be, regardless of the way I was fathered.   ___ ___

Intergenerational Action Plan

List five positive things you have learned from your father that you
would like to pass on to your son.

1. _____

2. _____

3. _____

4. _____

5. _____

Pick the most important of those five things and write down three
things you can do this week to begin to build that quality into your
son. In subsequent weeks do the same with the four remaining
qualities.

Action Steps

1. _____

2. _____

3. _____

The Heart of the Matter

...the fathering strength of time together

Andy DeJong is the pastor of Covenant Life Church in Grand Haven, Michigan. If the name sounds familiar it is because Andy is my boss, the senior pastor at my church. Andy, forty-seven, is married and the father of a son and a daughter, both of whom are in high school. Joel DeJong is a sixteen-year-old junior at Grand Rapids Christian High School.

Roger Bergman is the owner of two retail shoe stores. Forty-eight years old, he is married and the father of two sons, Nick and Bryce. Bryce, a seventeen-year-old senior in high school, works with his dad at their stores.

It is not easy to say which fathering strength is the most important or which one we should work on the most. All of the strengths are vital and enrich our relationship with our sons in different ways. But in our research with fathers and sons, we found that nearly every father and son had the strength of time together. This strength is absolutely necessary to building a strong relationship. Think about it. How do we build friendships with other people? We do things with them. We ask them out for dinner, or we play racquetball or golf with them, or we go to movies with them. We share our lives with them by giving them time. If we want to build

35

an enduring friendship with our sons, we need to do the same for them. Friendships are built on shared experiences, so we need to take time to be with our kids if we hope to build a strong, powerful relationship.

The question is, How do we do that? Let's look closely at the definition of time together. *Time together is simply a quantity of time in which there are opportunities for quality experiences and mutual satisfaction.* Examining that definition further, we see that first of all it is *a quantity of time.* It doesn't happen in five minutes a day or in an hour a week. There has to be significant volume, or relationship-building through shared experiences won't happen. Second, *time together requires quality experiences.* Sometimes these experiences require planning; sometimes they happen spontaneously. Rarely do they happen with a newspaper in front of our faces.

My father always has been a tremendous reader. He reads everything he can get his hands on because his desire to learn and grow is nearly insatiable. I remember a few times growing up when it seemed that his books were more important than I was. One time my brother and I decided to take matters into our hands. My dad kept a stack of books by his favorite chair, so every time he sat down, there was reading material for him. After my father fell asleep in his chair, my brother and I carefully and stealthily removed all of the books from around his chair, carried them into my bedroom, unceremoniously dumped them to the floor, and shoved them under the bed. When Dad woke up from his nap, his books and magazines were gone, and there were two smiling boys trying a little too hard not to look guilty. My dad, who knew a secret smile when he saw one, called us over. "OK, boys, where are my books?" he asked. "I need to study." "But Dad, we need to be with you. Read later, please?" My brother, who couldn't stand to get into trouble, ran into my room and brought his books down. Dad pulled us up on his lap and said, "Guys, I'm sorry if it seems like my stuff is more important than you. The truth is that you mean more to me than anything in the world. But I'm a pastor, and reading and studying are a part of my job. I'll tell you what. If you let me study for another hour, I'll put my books down after that and play baseball with you guys. What do you think? Will that work?" We smiled, agreed, and left him alone for that hour. When the clock hit 4 he walked out of the house, his glove on his hand, ready to play. My father kept his promise.

I asked my dad many years later about that incident. I wanted to know if he even remembered it. "Yeah, Jack, it's funny you should bring that story up," he said, "because I'll never forget what happened that day. I remember it as though it were yesterday. I felt like I had been hit on the head with a 2 x 4. 'Wake up, Schreur, your kids need you. Your books can wait.' That was a turning point for me. In a way, on that afternoon I decided that nothing would ever get in the way of my spending time with you again. And I've tried to live up to that."

I think about those words when I'm writing and my son comes banging on my office door. Or when we're home together but the football game is calling me at that same time my son is. *The second part of time together involves opportunities for quality experiences,* and that means we must put the paper down, turn off the television, and leave some work at the office. You don't get many quality experiences without planning for them, creating opportunities for them, and leaving space in your life for them.

The third component of time together involves mutual satisfaction. So often we believe that because we are watching the football game and our son is sitting on our lap, we are building our relationship by spending time together. That may be true, but it also may be true that my son doesn't like football and is sitting on my lap because it is the only way to be with me. The fathering strength of time together is bigger than that. We must learn what our sons like, what they want to do, what brings them joy, and then we must find ways to spend time with them doing not just what we want to do, but what they want to do. The words are *mutual satisfaction* — that means both of us are having fun and enjoying ourselves.

The three parts of the definition for time together can burden us. Many of us feel overwhelmed already with the responsibilities at our jobs, with our wives, and from other things that press our time. We wonder if we can find the ways to be involved creatively in our son's life. Not all of us believe that time together will work in our relationships with our sons. We may believe that we are too different from our boys, that we don't enjoy doing the same things, and that building shared experiences is only a pipe dream. Andy and Joel DeJong's story is instructive for us in this regard.

Andy and Joel, while they share some important similarities, are different in many key ways. Joel enjoys athletics; Andy doesn't. Andy likes nothing more than to spend time with other people, listening to them, getting them to open up their lives to him. Joel is quiet and reserved. He keeps his thoughts to himself and carefully thinks through every word he says. Although they are different people and have had difficult times (as many of the fathers and sons we talked with have had), they have built a strong relationship. Andy characterizes their friendship this way: "Although we struggle, I think we have, underlying it all, a deep and abiding love for each other and a sense of appreciation for each other. I believe that Joel at any time can be asked, 'Does your father, in fact, love you in spite of this garbage?' And he would answer, 'Yes.' That is what I believe about him as well." Joel, in typically understated fashion, looks at his father, looks at me, and says, "It's true. That's how I feel."

Joel and Andy forged their relationship, a friendship that transcends their differences, primarily by spending time together. They exhibit many of the fathering strengths, but time together stands out in their lives because they have worked so hard to create opportunities to be together.

"Joel and I are very different people," Andy says. "I'm not particularly athletic. . . ." Joel laughs quietly at this point. His father continues, "OK, I'm not really athletic *at all*, and so even though I encouraged Joel to pursue athletics, I didn't end up doing that with him a lot. That's just not me. I had to search to find things that Joel and I could enjoy together. We spent many years in Colorado, and Joel and I discovered that we liked to hike, and we spent a lot of time doing that together.

"This summer we spent time together, just Joel and I, driving out to Washington State, where I spoke at a conference. We spent some time hiking in Washington, and on the way home we spent a week hiking the Windriver Range in Wyoming.

"Another significant experience that Joel and I had was when he was in the fifth grade and we spent seven weeks in Africa together, just the two of us. That was an intense time because we were together all the time, every day for seven weeks, almost twenty-four hours a day. We were dependent on each other. We were each other's best friend and confidant. And even though Joel was only eleven, there was a sense that he was looking out for me."

What happens when Andy and Joel are together for these extended periods of time is interesting. They don't necessarily talk to each other a lot. They don't immediately dive into questions about the fate of the universe. They often spend hours without saying a single word. But their time together immeasurably strengthens their relationship.

"For some reason," Andy relates, "there is a territory that we each end up protecting when we're home, whereas the territory when we're in the van driving or when we're in the mountains is a shared territory, shared space for us." Joel continues, "We know that if we get into a fight in the mountains, there's no one else — it's just us. So if we get mad at each other, then that's it, because there is no one else to talk to. We spent all that time together this summer and didn't have a single fight."

Andy and Joel have discovered that when they are hiking or traveling together, they are having too much fun to fight about the things that often drag them down at home. They enjoy being together, building their friendship through shared experiences. And their times alone together are a point of contact for them for when they do get angry with each other, when they disagree about what is right and wrong, or when they just aren't getting along. They always have something to talk about because they have done so many things together. And when Joel is angry with his father for lecturing, or for punishing him, or for not understanding him, he can remember when they watched the bear in the Windriver Range, when he described the beauty of the wildflowers to his color-blind father. He can remember when his father reached out his hand to help him climb a steep rock face and when they were alone and afraid together in Uganda.

They have this strength in their relationship because Andy made it a priority. "I grew up never knowing my father, who today is eighty-three. I still do not know him. My greatest longing growing up was to know how he felt. I said to myself at some point, 'If I ever have children, I'm going to let them know who I am.' By spending time with Joel, I'm trying to communicate with him who I am and what is important to me. I travel with Joel because I really want to experience new places and adventures with him. When I took Joel to Africa, he was old enough to appreciate it. I didn't want to go alone. I wanted to be with Joel, and I wanted him to have that experience to enrich his life."

Andy and Joel accomplish their time together through special events, like a hiking vacation, a trip, or just a night out to the movies together. But most of us won't have chances to travel with our sons to Africa, so the opportunities to build shared experiences will have to happen in more ordinary, perhaps mundane ways. We will have to figure out how to build time together while trying to pay the mortgage, feed the kids, and still get to work on time. That isn't an easy task, but it can be done.

Roger and Bryce Bergman are two of the quietest people I know. They aren't exuberant or outrageous. But in living their lives quietly, they have built a unique and wonderful friendship. And they have done it largely by using the one thing that none of us can escape: work. With this simple thing in common they are building an enduring and strong relationship.

"I've made a point to work on my relationship with my boys," Roger says. "Nick and Bryce are important to me, and I feel that it is important to stay close to them and spend time with them. So when they are in school, I try to have breakfast out with them, about once every week or every couple of weeks. It gives me an opportunity to check into their lives and find out what's happening—to get to know them a little bit." Bryce adds, "I like it because some days—or some weeks—it can get real busy at the store, and if he's been working every night, I might go to bed before he gets home and I don't see much of him. But when we go out for breakfast, it's just him and me, and, well . . ." he adds with a smile, "the food is good."

Now a senior in high school, Bryce works all summer and

during the weekends with his dad. It gives them an opportunity to be together and learn about each other. Roger says, "We have fun together at work. We work with great people and enjoy our time together. We also compete in a friendly way, and Bryce does a very good job of competing with me. Sometimes he beats me. I treat him with respect; he treats me with respect."

Roger and Bryce didn't build their mutual respect overnight. They built it by spending a great deal of time together. Roger has taken a potential negative — his many hours on the job — and has turned it into a strength of their relationship. He was able to do that because he realized that in order to build a relationship with his sons and make a living, he would have to combine the two somehow. So he asks Bryce to accompany him when he goes to the big sportswear convention in Chicago. Granted, it's easier to go alone, but he wants to spend time with his son. Bryce remembers another special time with his dad: "December 7, 1990, Chicago Stadium. My dad took me to a Bulls game. That was awesome!" Roger continues the story, "We had a good time. I'd gotten some great tickets from one of our salesmen. We were in the tenth row, or close to it. It was a great night."

It would have been easy for Roger to invite some of his close friends to go see Michael Jordan light it up. It might even have been more fun for him, but Roger wanted Bryce to become one of his close friends and realized that wouldn't happen without some shared experiences. He knew how much Bryce would remember the game, so he gave the tickets — and more importantly his time — to his son.

Bryce and Roger have a special relationship, but they are not so different from many of us. They still struggle and have difficult times, but the time they spend together has enabled them to build an incredible amount of respect for each other, and that respect has carried them almost entirely through Bryce's adolescence. Their relationship isn't just intact, it's growing stronger. In Bryce's words, "I feel lucky. Sometimes I see that some of my friends have parents who just don't care enough about them to even ask how they are doing, and they treat their kids like . . . kids. But it's nice with my dad. He gives me respect and space but takes the time to

41

be with me. I see it usually at the store, when we're together, but at home too."

"The key element for me has been spending time with Nick and Bryce," Roger remarks. "Spending time in prayer for them and with them and being with them, making sure that we're still connected. I work a lot of hours. I'm gone at least a couple of nights a week, plus a night or two working at church. But I've tried to include them in my life in as many ways as I can. I think of all those breakfasts that we have had together, and a lot of times there's not much conversation because it's early. Sometimes we don't say much, and I understand that. We quietly eat our breakfast and then go to work and have a good day."

The Myths of Time Together

There are two myths that can distort the idea of time together. They have become prominent because many fathers realize that they don't spend sufficient time with their sons. So instead of changing their fathering pattern, they change the definition of time together or water it down through these myths.

The first myth is widespread in our society — *the myth of quality time.* This myth tells us that we don't have to spend a lot of time with our sons as long as it is quality time. Some research shows that the average American father spends less than seven minutes per day in meaningful interaction with his children. Is that real quality time? We rationalize that maybe we aren't a constant part of our sons' lives, but we do special things with them that compensate for the lack of actual hours spent with them. Maybe we take them to the ballgame once a year or to Disney World every fall, and we believe that will accomplish the same thing as spending hours and hours with our sons on a consistent basis. That just isn't true. We can't program quality. Quality only happens *within* a quantity of time.

It is hard to understand how we can hide behind this myth. It should be obvious that one pro baseball game a year doesn't make up for missing every Little League game. One hour of heart-to-heart talking doesn't replace tens of hours of sitting together. This myth is a product of our guilt. We know that our children deserve better of us, but it is easier for many of us to work than to be with our sons. It is easier to spend time with our friends than to search for common ground with our boys. We feel guilty, and this myth lets us off the hook.

When my brother and I were eleven and twelve years old, respectively, my dad took us on a camping and fishing trip to Canada. We drove almost fourteen hours one way to get to our spot, and then we camped and fished for three straight days, just the three of us. Not even the fish interrupted us! We didn't catch a single thing. We didn't even see a fish. We tried every form of bait known to man, but the fish spurned our offerings. As a fishing excursion, that trip was a total failure. As a father-son relationship builder, it was a terrific success.

During those five days together we talked about everything under the sun. Most of the time we talked about meaningless and transitory things. Occasionally, though, our conversations would go deeper, and my father would have a chance to get to know us and for us to know him. Why did that happen? Because we were spending such a huge quantity of time together. Out of the seventy-odd hours we were awake and together, we spent about two hours in real, honest sharing. But the only reason we were able to spend those two hours in sharing was because of the other seventy hours. My dad could not have programmed those two hours of deep communication, of true quality time. They happened only within the framework of lots of time together. That trip is one of the best memories of my childhood. It was when I reconnected with my father. It was the beginning of my adolescence, and it set the tone for my relationship with my dad through my teen years.

The myth that we can program quality time exclusive of a quantity of time is ultimately dispiriting. We try to program a half a day here and an hour there, and we become frustrated when our children don't respond the way we want them to respond. We give up, feeling that our kids don't really want to be with us anyway, so why try? We cannot state this principle strongly enough: if you desire quality time with your son, you must allocate a large quantity of time to him.

43

The second myth that distorts our idea of time together is *the myth of make-up time.* In this myth we believe that we can put off time with our sons now, and later when they are older and more mature, or more interesting and our lives are less busy, we will spend time with them. That just doesn't happen. Why will your sons want to be with you in five or ten years when you don't want to be with them now? What will draw them to you during their early adulthood when you aren't spending time with them during their early adolescence? Why will your teenage sons want to be with you when you haven't spent time with them as younger children?

The movie *Hook* illustrates this idea very well. *Hook* is Steven Spielberg's spirited retelling of the story of Peter Pan, and in this movie Peter has grown up to become a lawyer and corporate raider. He has forgotten who he really is. At one point in the movie Peter misses his son's baseball game after promising to be there; an "important meeting" held him up. On the way to London, Peter's son Jack draws a picture of an airplane going down in flames. Everyone in the family escapes with a parachute except Dad. He is free-falling out of the plane. Peter sits next to his son and asks why he alone doesn't have a parachute. His son tells him that he's angry at him for missing his game after he had promised to be there. "I promise Jackie," Peter says. "I'll go to six games next year, scout's honor. My word is my bond." His son looks at him, then looks away and says, "Yeah, junk bonds."

Many of us are in danger of our promises being seen in the same way. "I'll play with you later, Son." But later never seems to come. "I'll be home from work in an hour, and we can work on your curveball then." Then an important phone call holds us up, and it's dark by the time we get home. The myth of make-up time robs us of time with our sons *now*. The myth tells us that if we build our businesses now, we can be with our kids later. We'll make it up to them. The myth tells us that if we break one of our promises or even a dozen promises now, we can make it up to them later. After all, they will understand. Our boys know that we are busy trying to provide a living for the family. They know that the reason we're gone so much is because we're trying to make their lives better. At least that is how the conversation in our minds goes. But the truth is that often all our kids want is us, and we are not there.

My dad tells the story of a man he was counseling. A successful small-business owner, this guy had worked sixty to seventy hours per week for twenty years. He sat in my dad's office, however, far from the model of the successful businessman. His wife had left, and his two sons wanted nothing to do with him. He buried his face in his hands. "All I ever wanted was to make their lives better than mine had been. And you know what they said to me last night? 'We never wanted your stuff, Dad. All we wanted was you.' "

The Bible asks, "What good is it for a man to gain the whole world, yet forfeit his soul?" (Mark 8:36) Our question is, "What does it profit a man to gain the whole world and lose his son?" The idea that we can make up time with our sons is false. Our sons are only what they are at this moment, for this moment. They will never be six again or sixteen again. Once this moment is gone it is gone, irretrievably lost, and if we haven't spent this moment with our sons, then both we and they are poorer for it.

If you want to build a friendship with your sons, you need to start by enjoying them wherever they are at this moment. If your sons are babies and you don't know what to do with babies, learn how to change a diaper. Take the time to give them a bath, to hold them as they go to sleep. They will never be babies again. You can't ever make up the time you'll lose with them. They'll never be that soft; their breath will never have that slight Elmer's Glue smell again. It happens only when they are babies.

Our encouragement to you is to stop putting off being with your sons. Take advantage of the opportunities you have right now. Don't wait until some predetermined point in the future. Your boys need you right now, and you need them.

Four Keys To Spending Time Together

There are four simple, practical things we can do to make our time with our sons relationship-building experiences. First, *we need to provide for both mundane and extraordinary experiences.* I spent time with my father almost every day of my life. He took me to the hardware store with him, to the gas station, and to the garage. He asked me to hold the flashlight when he was working on the car, and I chased down the 9/16ths socket or wrench when it was needed. It may not have seemed like much to him, but it was incredibly special to me. The mundane, ordinary times in his life became a point of contact for us and built our relationship.

My father also took the time occasionally to do the extraordinary with us. We went on trips to Chicago together. Sometimes he took my brother; sometimes he took me. But we always did something special when we were there. One Sunday after he had spoken in a church in the Chicago area, he took me on a helicopter tour of the city. It was an extraordinary, wonderful experience for me, and it has been a reference point in our lives. To this day, almost twenty years later, not a month passes that we don't talk about that trip to Chicago and how much fun we had.

I know you are busy, and time is the currency of the nineties. We are asking you to invest some of that currency in your boys' lives. Include them in your daily routine. And once or twice a year spend extraordinary time with them. The stories in this chapter have borne out this point. Roger and Bryce have built their relationship largely on the ordinary things of life: working together, eating together, riding in the car together. Andy and Joel have done that as well, but they illustrate the importance of occasionally taking the time and resources to have an extraordinary experience with your sons.

The second way we can enrich our time together is through questioning and listening. Some of us are good interrogators: "Where have you been? What have you done? Who were you with?" But that isn't what is meant here. Instead, when you are with your son, ask him open-ended questions that require some thought to answer, and then listen carefully to his answers.

For example, when riding in the car together for a long period of time, ask your teenage son what his fondest memory of his childhood is and why. Then listen to him closely. By listening to his answers, you will occasionally get a glimpse into his soul, and you will learn more about him in five minutes than you had in the last five months. Don't play Twenty Questions. Just think of a few, important things you want to talk about and ask away. Give your son the freedom to not answer, and realize that this kind of exercise can't happen twenty-four hours a day. Give him the opportunity to tell you about his hopes, dreams, loves, and fears by asking him the right questions and then listening closely for the answers.

The third principle that will help us enjoy our time together with our children is to make some of the time we spend together regular and consistent. Roger and Bryce meet once a week for breakfast. That time is important to Bryce because it is a regular, consistent point of contact with his dad. Joel and his dad regularly go to see a movie together. My son and I regularly go out to eat together. Establishing some regular, non-stressful time together can enrich your relationship in powerful ways. The consistency and regularity prove to your son that you are serious about him and serious about wanting to be with him. Setting aside every other Wednesday, for example, says a great deal about your priorities in life and speaks volumes to your son.

The fourth way we can deepen our time together is by having both "alone time" and "together time." Make sure some of the time you spend with your son is for just the two of you. No other distractions, nobody else's agenda, just the two of you. But some of the time you spend together should be in concert with the rest of the family or with his friends. Invite him to take a friend along when you go some place with him. Involve the whole family in an extraordinary experience. Be sure to use both types of time together.

Being alone with your son is an opportunity to speak about quiet, even hidden things. It is your chance to say that you love him and to hear him say he loves you. It is imperative to build some alone-time with your son. But in together-time you get a chance to see how he interacts with his friends. Is he a leader or a follower? Is he confident, shy, commanding? Only by observing him with others will you get that glimpse into his life.

When planning time with your son, include opportunities for both kinds of time together to give you a complete picture of your son and a variety of shared experiences.

We've been strong in our assertion that spending time together is not negotiable. If you don't do it, you won't be able to build a strong friendship that will last a lifetime. Time together won't happen until you plan it and follow through with your plan. Don't miss the boat on this one. Don't gain the whole world and lose your son because everything else seemed more important. Purpose this day to build your relationship with your son by spending time with him, letting him know that you care about him enough to be with him.

Time-Together Checklist

	Often	Sometimes	Seldom
1. My son and I schedule playtimes together.	___	___	___
2. We allow work and other activities to infringe on our planned time together.	___	___	___
3. We plan how to use our time.	___	___	___
4. We are spontaneous and respond to opportunities for play and fun.	___	___	___
5. Our family controls/limits television usage.	___	___	___
6. We prioritize our activities.	___	___	___

7. We don't overschedule
   activities that are outside
   the family.   ____   ____   ____

8. I feel guilty about spending
   free time playing or having
   fun with my son.   ____   ____   ____

Time-Together Action Plan

Activities:
(Working with your son list the things you can or would like to do together)

_____

_____

_____

_____

_____

_____

Family members or friends included:

_____

_____

_____

Where, When, How:

_____

_____

_____

_____

We, _____, father and son, pledge to spend _____ time together this next year. We believe that time together is important, and we promise not to let the demands of life prevent us from being together.

Next week we will _____.

Next month we will _____.

Next year we will _____.

Signed: _____ and _____

Chapter Four

Be All You Can Be

...the fathering strength of commitment

Dan Cummings is the pastor at a rapidly growing church. At thirty-eight he is youthful, energetic, and talented—one of the most gifted preachers we have ever heard. We caught up to Dan on a Thursday, a special day in his family. On Thursdays his oldest son, Benjamin (four years old), spends the day at work with Dad. When we interviewed Dan about his relationship with his two sons, Benjamin and Braden (two), Ben was climbing the ladder in his father's library, hanging out with his dad.

Ed Nienhuis is a businessman, and a good one. As the vice president for a large chain of retail stores, he spends his days on corporate jets and in corporate suites. He is used to telling others what to do and having them do it. His son, Luke, is a student at Calvin College, with an earring and fashionably long or short hair (depending on the month). Luke is very much his own person, pursuing his own dreams. They seem to be an odd couple, but through commitment to each other they have built a strong and lasting friendship that transcends their differences.

As I sit down and begin to write this chapter, my mind is buzzing with the popular advertisement for the United States Army. The ubiquitous song goes, "Be all that you can be, get an

51

edge on life . . . in the Army!" The images that accompany the music feature strong, well-disciplined young men driving tanks, jumping out of airplanes, rappelling down the sheer face of a cliff, and performing other very "manly" skills. The phrase may be somewhat overused, but it really describes the fathering strength of commitment. Fathers who are truly committed to their sons want them to be all they can be, and they do their best to help their sons reach their potential.

Commitment is about caring enough for your son that your goal in life becomes helping him achieve his goals. Commitment means putting his needs above yours sometimes. To reach a high level of commitment with your son and to inspire the same commitment in him means to reach a level of friendship, trust, and selflessness that will propel the two of you for many years. This fathering strength incorporates many of the others. For instance, it is impossible to build commitment without building trust and respect. Commitment does not happen without time together and many other fathering strengths. But it is difficult to have many of those other fathering strengths in your relationship without commitment.

A television sitcom character defined the difficulty of a committed father-son relationship very well recently. This father was divorced and a recovering alcoholic. He took his eleven-year-old boy to live with him on a trial, two-week basis. After one week he returned his son to his ex-wife, defeated and feeling like a failure. "It's harder than I thought," he told her. "When I go to bed he is there. And when I wake up he is there. And all day he is there, and he's looking at me like he's waiting for me to say something to him or to do something with him." The struggling father went on, "My girlfriend called and wanted to go out, but my son wanted me to help him with his homework. Heck, I don't know what to do. It's just that he needs me so much. I can't do it!"

Though spoken by a fictional television character, those words speak for many of the fathers in this country. Commitment is hard, because being committed to another person is an inherently unselfish act. It means putting that person first, encouraging him, challenging him, helping him, to quote our Army slogan again, "Be all he can be." Commitment is not an easy strength to develop in our relationships. But the results of developing commitment are enormous, and after you hear from the fathers and sons we interviewed you'll agree with us. Commitment is tough, but it is worth it.

How do you develop commitment in your relationship? How is this elusive trait built into fathers' and sons' lives? How can we make it a part of our relationship? These questions can be answered in part by telling you about Dan Cummings.

Dan is relatively new to fathering sons; his oldest is only four. But Dan already exhibits a commitment to his two young sons that would be the envy of almost any father. "I want to enjoy everything about my boys. I want to know them inside and out. They both have wonderful personalities. And I want them to know me too, to know what I do and why I do it," Dan says.

"I want to enjoy their uniqueness and not to try to bend them or fit them into a mold they don't fit. I want them to grasp God's parameters for their lives. I've taken it as literal that curriculum isn't written by Scripture Press or Gospel Light. The curriculum for my children is written by God and is called life. It is what they experience. I want to be there to interpret it for them or with them. I want to be there to constantly show them God's perspective, how God thinks, how God reacts. I want them to have the mind of God about them, and I can't do that if, number one, I'm not there and number two, if I have some kind of manufactured grid I'm trying to shove them into. It is really about living together every day, and as we live together I try to show them God and try to help them think about that.

"The issue for me is not what we do together, but that we get to be together, that my boys get to be with Dad. I want my children to be very comfortable with the landscape of my job, so they have grown up coming to the office, playing here. Every Thursday Benjamin comes to my office. He spends all day here with me, hanging out, climbing the ladder and the bookshelves, playing in the playroom in the nursery. We go to lunch. We hike around the church property. He just hangs out with me. And he knows every Thursday that happens. He has access to me all the time."

There are two keys to developing commitment in our relationships with our sons. The first key is demonstrated very well by

Dan Cummings. It is *knowledge*. If we want to develop commitment, if want to help our kids reach their potential, becoming the men that God intends them to be, we need to know our sons and they need to know us. That is why Dan brings his son to work with him on Thursdays. That is why he spends so much time with him. That is why he is a committed dad—he knows his boys. If we want to live as committed fathers, we need to know our own sons. Getting to know our sons takes more than just asking them how their day was. It involves at least the following three things:

1. *Observing them*

2. *Understanding them*

3. *Listening to them*

When we take the time to do these things we will get to know our children, and in knowing them we will be able to encourage them as they follow their dreams. We will be able to help them develop their gifts and talents. We will be able to see the possibilities for their lives.

Observing Our Sons

I was intently going over some research for this book when I heard my wife calling my name. She was only about three feet away but evidently had been trying to get my attention for quite some time. "Jack, you've got to come outside and see your son. He's been calling for you for about ten minutes. He wants to show you something." "Just a couple of minutes, Leslie. I'm almost done here," I replied, and returned to my work. I looked up again about an hour later and realized that I had forgotten to check on Jonathon. I ran outside, but nobody was in the yard. I checked around the house, but my family had quietly deserted me. When they returned about a half-hour later, I asked Leslie what had happened. "Well, Jack, we got tired of waiting for you and went to the store." "But what about Jay [Jonathon]? What was he going to show me?" I asked. "Hey, you had your chance and missed it." Leslie said it with a smile, but I knew she was telling me something important. I wasn't paying attention to my son. I had stopped watching him and other things had caught my eye.

How many times has that happened to you? It is simple to instruct fathers to observe their sons, but we don't do it. The game on TV calls us, or our work is too pressing or too important to put down. And when we finally look up, the moment is gone and we have missed it. If we want to build a committed relationship with our sons, we need to take time to just observe them. We need to watch them as they go about their lives. We need to notice how they handle conflict. We need to learn what they are interested in by watching them play. We need to get to know their friends — not to judge them but to better see our own children. Observation means putting aside what we want to see, our beliefs about what our sons are or aren't, and watching their lives to see what is really going on.

Observation takes concentration and discipline, but through it you will learn volumes about your son. Don't make the mistake of letting everything else preoccupy you so that you miss what is truly important. Take the time (and it will take lots of time) to observe your son.

Understanding Our Sons

It is one thing to observe, but as scientists prove throughout the ages, it is quite another to understand. If we are to build committed relationships we must understand our sons. We need to understand their strengths, their weaknesses, their potentials, and their problems. We need to understand what motivates them and what discourages them. We need to get an occasional glimpse into their souls. *Easier said than done,* you may be thinking, and you are right. But just because understanding our sons isn't easy doesn't make it impossible. We can do some simple things to understand our sons, to get a peek into their souls. First, pay attention to the popular culture your son consumes. If he watches TV at all, note what he watches and then ask him about it. Don't be judgmental.

Just ask him what he likes about a particular show or character. Monitor the movies he goes to see and the ones he brings home. We miss a golden opportunity to understand our children when we drop them off at the Cineplex and have no idea which of the eight movies playing they are going to see; if we ask them what they are going to do on any given night and they reply, "Watch a video," and we fail to ask which video.

Popular culture also includes music, and perhaps this is where you will get the clearest window into your child's soul. What does he listen to and why? Is it music of alienation? Oldies? Plain old rock and roll? Is your son into alternative, heavy metal, or country? Whom does he like the most and why? Ask him these questions and be very brave: listen to his music and get to know it. Not so that you can judge it and ban it from the house (although that may be a real and valid impulse), but to know what is influencing your son. The popular culture your son consumes (and *consume* is the right word for it) is part of what is making him, and if you yearn to understand him you will pay attention to that aspect of his life.

Understanding our sons when they are younger takes time. It means observing them and then interpreting your observations. How does your son interact with his friends? Why do you think he responds that way? Talk to your son, even your two- or three-year-old, and ask him what is going on. Ask him about his friends, his school, his teacher, his day, and then try to put yourself in his Reeboks, so to speak. What is it like to be him? What are his fears and joys? Only through asking these questions over and over will we begin to understand our sons.

Understanding your son also means trying to figure out the reasons behind the actions, and depending on where your child is developmentally, that may drive you to distraction. If you have a teenage son this is a difficult task, but no less valuable because of its difficulty. If you have a young son it may be as simple as asking him, "Why did you do that?" The key is to find whatever means you can to understand your son. Because when you understand him you will be able to help him reach his potential, to help him become the person God wants him to become.

Listening to Our Sons

The final component to getting to know your son is perhaps the most difficult one. Listening to our sons, no matter how old they are, takes practice. It means we not only hear the words but we also pay attention to their tone, their body language, and their mood. It means that we listen to their emotions, which are sometimes displayed inappropriately. Instead of reacting angrily we must listen.

Although I work with families for a living and spend a great deal of time listening to other fathers' sons, I struggle to listen to my own son. I don't know how many times a day Jonathon has to call me four or five times before I respond to him. I can't count the times in a week that he is talking to me, telling me something about his life, and my mind is on this book or a problem at church. I simply don't discipline myself enough to listen to his small, somewhat hesitant voice. And when I fail to listen to him I am not building commitment.

In doing the research for this book my dad and I must have heard fifty sons say the equivalent of, "My dad wasn't perfect and we struggled, but he listened to me and that made all the difference." My guess is that Dan Cummings' sons will utter similar words in the years to come, because Dan is committed to his sons and listens to them. So what should we do? We need to commit ourselves to using the mute button on the remote control for our TVs. I'm serious. When our sons come into the room and the game is in the fourth quarter and the score is tight, hit the mute button and listen to your son when he speaks to you. Put down the newspaper and look into his eyes. Let him know by nodding your head occasionally that you are actively a part of the conversation, that what he has to say is important. We spend a great deal of time talking about listening in chapter 8. Suffice it to say that you can't build a committed relationship without knowledge of your son, and you will never know him until you listen to him.

Invest Your Life in Your Son

Build commitment into your relationship with your son by investing in his life. Some of us are familiar with stocks, bonds, and mutual funds. We take care of our resources and invest them wisely. But this is a little different; fathers need to invest their resources in their sons. I'm not talking about money or property. No, this investment involves *us:* our time, our energies, our emotional, physical, and spiritual resources, and our presence.

All of us have intangible resources that we allocate to what is important. I like to play golf, so I allocate a certain part of my time to playing and practicing. Along with that I allocate some mental resources in thinking through my game, how can I play better. I read books and magazine articles to become a better golfer. I also invest emotional resources into the game. When you consider my skill level (low), I invest too much emotionally into every round of golf. I care about every stroke, and I want each one to be perfect. As fathers we need to invest in our sons' lives in the same way. We need to give everything we have to the relationship and to care about the outcome.

One of the fine lines that committed fathers walk is the line between investing in our sons' lives and interfering in them. Sometimes when we care deeply about our boys and put a great deal of time and thought into fathering, we believe that investment gives us the right to run their lives, or at least to have a big say. Committed fathers find a balance between investment and interference. They are in their kids' lives, but they don't dominate them. Good committed fathers are available to their sons but don't do for them what their sons can do for themselves.

A good example of this is Ed and Luke Nienhuis. Ed has invested a great deal into his relationship with his son, Luke. But Ed has also let the free-thinking Luke be himself. He has given him the foundation of their friendship and the freedom to move beyond it.

Luke remembers vacations together in Gulf Shores, Alabama, and sailing on their sailboat. "We did a lot of stuff together," Luke says. "We even went to Europe together."

"Every few years Luke's school would go to Europe with the soccer team, and when it was Luke's turn to go I volunteered to be one of the parents that went along," Ed recalls.

"I let him come, but at first I wasn't real big on the idea. Then I thought about it and said, 'That's OK. That's cool. I can handle it. He was OK," Luke adds.

"We did the trip together but separately, if you know what I mean," Ed says. "He kind of stayed with his friends and I stayed with the adults, and we did lots of things together as a group." Luke chimes in with a smile on his face, "When money was involved we were together, and for other things we were separate."

"When you went into Paris for a night on the town, Luke, we were apart. But I trusted you, even though we waited up for you. We were in Paris, near downtown, and you had to take the last subway back. So all of the adults were sitting in the lobby looking at our watches, thinking if you missed this train you would probably never come home. But all of a sudden the train pulled in, and you made it home."

"You never asked what went on, Dad, but I think you kind of had an idea."

"I trusted you, Luke."

Spending time with Ed and Luke reminded me what real commitment is all about. Ed couldn't stop talking about his son's achievements, to the point where I think it embarrassed Luke. Ed's joy in raising his son came from helping Luke become all he could be. And in helping Luke reach his potential, Ed invested a great deal into the relationship, but he also knew how to let Luke live his own life.

"Anything Luke was involved in we were there," Ed says. "The key is that we were all kind of sharing the same stuff without getting in each other's way, so we could all do our own thing, but do it together." I asked Luke whether his father's constant presence in his life — at his soccer games, at the track meets, even going with him to Europe — bothered him. "It was OK. It didn't bother me at all. Like the trip to Europe. I guess that is one of those times when you're not supposed to be hanging out with your parents. But it was good. It didn't phase me at all. I appreciated having my dad at my games. I was surprised he was able to come to so many. But he does make a point of letting me be, of trying not to get too much into my life. Why he does that I don't know. I think we have an understanding."

"I'll tell you why I do that with Luke," Ed interjects. "He's got his head screwed on right. He's a smart guy. He's got it together. I believe in him."

Ed and Luke give you an idea of what a committed relationship looks like. You realize the investment of time and energy that a busy guy like Ed has made in Luke's life. You feel that Ed's presence has been a stabilizing influence on Luke, but not an overbearing one. You can sense how much pride Ed feels for his son and the appreciation his son feels for him.

Our investment in our son's life has to happen in these three key areas:

1. Our time and energy

2. Our emotional resources

3. Our presence

Time and Energy

Everyone has time and energy. We don't all have the same amount of money; some of us are more skilled at certain things than others; but all of us have time and energy. I can hear the protests now: "But you haven't seen my schedule, Jack. You don't realize how busy I am." The truth is that we all have the same amount of time. The key is in the allocation of that time. How you prioritize your time and energy tells your son what matters most to you in life. If you spend most of your time working, your son will begin to understand that work is the most important thing in your life. If you spend most of your free time apart from your son, he will understand his place in your life.

I knew early on what my place was in my father's life. The way he allocated his time showed me exactly what was important. My father began his ministry in a small church near Chicago. He was young, it was his first pastorate, and my brother and I were in elementary school. As the only pastor he was a busy man. He married, buried, called on the sick; he taught Sunday School, preached twice on Sundays, and led the obligatory midweek prayer meeting. Yet one of my earliest memories is coming home from school when I was in the second grade. I crossed the small yard that separated our house (the parsonage) from the little church, walked into his office at church, and climbed on his lap. It was a beautiful fall day, typical of the Midwest in the middle of October. The sun was shining, the temperature was unseasonably warm, and I wanted to play catch with my dad. "Dad, whatcha doing?" "I'm getting ready for my message this Sunday, Jack, and I've still got a lot of work left to do." "Well, I want to play catch. Let's go." As a typical second-grader, I assumed the world revolved around me and my needs. But my father didn't dismiss me out of hand. He smiled at me and said, "Jack, I really want to play with you, but I'm in the middle of something right now. I tell you what. It's about 3:00 now. If you let me finish this, I promise I'll come out and play with you at 4:00." I left, and sure enough at 4:00 he was there, and we played catch and walked around the block together until dinnertime.

I knew that my dad thought I was important. I knew my place in his life was unassailable. I knew that his work, although very important to him, would never own his soul. I knew that I owned his soul and his heart. My father was committed to me and my brother, and he showed that commitment and built that commitment by investing his time and energy into our lives.

I am, unfortunately, a busy father as well. I am the pastor to youth and families at a growing church. I also am the director of Face to Face Ministries, and I spend a lot of time writing books and traveling and speaking. It is easy for me to pour my time and energy into my work. I love ministry and everything that I do. But at times I have invested too much into what I do and have left out my family. A few years ago I was confronted by my dad on this. He told me frankly that my kids and my wife were more important than my ministry, and that if I really believed what I said about them being the most important part of my life, then I had better put my time where my mouth was. He was honest with me and a little stern, and he was right.

I spend more time at home now, working out of a home office

so that even when I am in the middle of a project I can be with my family. We have invested heavily into video curriculum to cut down on the amount of speaking we were doing. I am now home three weekends out of four. I see my son every day. Each day I try to do something simple with just him, even going to the post office or shoveling snow from our driveway. I want to build a committed relationship with him, and I know that I have to invest my time and energy into his life if I hope to do that. So I have made the lifestyle choices to make sure that happens.

You probably don't have the flexibility that I am blessed with. It is hard for most men to tell their bosses that from now on they will be working at home. And it does take a great deal of time and energy to put food on the table for your family and a roof over their heads. But all of us still make choices about allocating the precious resource of time. Every day we decide whether we will spend ten minutes watching the news or reading with our sons. Every day we choose to get up ten minutes earlier and have breakfast out with our boys or to roll over and go back to sleep. All of us have the same amount of time. We need to decide how best to invest it in our sons' lives.

Emotional Resources

It is not just time and energy that we need to invest to build a committed relationship. We need to invest ourselves emotionally in our sons as well. We need to truly care about them and about the things they care about. This is one area where Ed Nienhuis excelled. When Luke became interested in soccer, Ed became interested in soccer. When Luke ran track, Ed was there cheering him on. Ed invested himself emotionally in his son's life and it paid off in commitment. Too many fathers are physically present but emotionally absent. Although they are home, their minds and hearts are still at work. If we want our sons to be all they can be, if we want to help them reach their potential, we need to invest ourselves emotionally in their lives.

What does that mean, and how does that work? It is the difference between being there and really *being there*, body and soul. My dad used to take me with him when he spoke in other churches. We would drive for hours together, and Dad invested himself emotionally into those times. He would ask about me. He found out what moved me and let it move him. He was *there* in every sense of that word. That is what it means to be emotionally invested in your son. And it is not possible to build a committed relationship with your son apart from that emotional investment.

Presence

Tied up in all of this, but so far unspoken or assumed, is the idea that we must invest our presence. We have to be with our sons. We told you earlier how we heard throughout our research for this book sons talking about their fathers being there. We have talked about this at length in chapter 3, but it needs to be said in this context as well. Helping your son achieve his potential cannot happen without you there. If you aren't around you can't do it, and you will not have a committed relationship. On the other hand, if you do commit to presence in your son's life, you can help him become the man that God wants him to be. It is that simple.

Your time is valuable. Invest it in your relationship with your son, and the dividend of commitment you will reap will bring joy to your life for years. Invest yourself emotionally in his life, and experience life though his eyes; find out what moves him, and let it move you. Your commitment to him will grow. Finally, invest your presence in your son. You have no idea how much it means to him that you are there for him.

When I was in junior high I played football for my school. I was one of the smallest kids on the team and was not a particularly good player. Every Saturday evening I would look into the stands and see my dad sitting there, and Saturday after Saturday I didn't play. Yet he was still there. Finally, in the next-to-last game of the season we were undefeated and were pummeling a visiting team. I was put into the game for the final two minutes as a defensive back. The runner came my way, and I managed to grab him by the shoe. Two other players joined in, and we managed to bring him down. I had shared in a tackle! I looked quickly to the stands and saw my father smiling, with his thumb pointed up in the air, sharing in my brief and modest moment of glory because he was committed to me.

Commitment Checklist

Check all of the following that are true of you and your son.

☐ 1. I feel strongly committed to my son and his welfare.

☐ 2. I often place my son's needs above my own.

☐ 3. I sense that I really know my son well.

☐ 4. I am aware of my son's behavior and interests.

☐ 5. My son would say that I am a good listener.

☐ 6. I believe that I am investing heavily in my son's life.

☐ 7. I am there for my son when he needs me.

If you were unable to check some of the above statements, stop and take a fresh look at your level of commitment to your son. Maybe some changes need to be made. Don't be afraid to say, "I have failed in this area, but I will do better." You can start fresh today. Tell your son that you want to be more involved in his life. Ask him for specific suggestions as to how this could begin to happen.

Chapter Five

Recess!

...the fathering strength
of play and laughter

Dave Claus is the president of a large continuing care retirement community. He is by everybody's estimation a good, responsible executive. But you wouldn't know that if all you had seen of Dave was the way he plays with his three boys, Bill, fourteen, Adam, eleven, and Danny, seven. They are an energetic and fun-loving bunch who understand the power of play in their relationship.

Tom and T.C. Cousineau have spent time hiking and roughing it since T.C. was a little boy. Now, helping his dad administer a Christian camp and enjoying the outdoors take up most of T.C.'s time. Tom, when he isn't teaching his son a new move while they're rock climbing, is building a successful year-round camping program as the executive director of Center Lake Bible Camp.

My son is in kindergarten. So far he has not shown the inclination to be the studious type. He may develop it, but right now his life is too full. He is too busy playing. Ask him what he likes most about school and he will yell, "Recess!" as he runs past on his way to yet another reenactment of a titanic battle between Spiderman and Batman. Jonathon lives his entire life as if it were recess.

Do you remember recess? That glorious time when the slowly ticking clock that kept you in class ad infinitum suddenly spun at

65

four times its normal rate? Do you remember the release of walking out from a spelling test to the playground, where for twelve glorious minutes you could do as you pleased? *Recess.* The word almost has a magic quality about it to American schoolchildren.

Ask almost any third-grader what he likes about school and he will echo Jonathon's response. Our kids know what makes life fun. They understand the value of recess. They understand that you can be serious only for so long and then you need a break. Our kids know that in the long run, recess is what really matters.

My brother dreads the annual job of renewing his license plates. It's not that it is a difficult ritual or too expensive. No, he dreads it because my father is unwilling to let Jon forget that he is, sometimes, a goofball. As a sophomore in college, my brother, newly wed and the proud owner of a 1975 green Chevrolet Impala, needed to renew his license for the car. In Michigan that involves purchasing tabs with the correct month and year and sticking them on the license plate. My brother, Mr. 4.0 who never got a B in high school, purchased his tabs and went out to the front of our house where his car was parked near my parents' car. Once applied, the stickers do not come off. They are made to stay on during hard Michigan winters and hot, steamy summers. Somehow my brother got confused and mistook my parents' bright-red Ford Escort for his green Impala and put his tabs on their car. My father watched the whole thing from the living room window and never said a word until my brother got back into the house. "Jon, thanks for buying tabs for my car. I needed them." "Yeah, sure, Dad. What are you talking about. . . ." My father began to laugh hysterically and point at his car. "Jonson, boy, you put your tabs on my car." My brother turned red, ran out to the cars, and checked his handiwork. When he came back in he asked for an Exacto knife and sheepishly joined in the laughter. How does a high school honors student confuse a green tank of a car with a small, red Escort? It is inexplicable, and every year around renewal time the story comes up. One year my brother asked, "Dad, if you watched me put them on the wrong car, why didn't you stop me?" "Because, my boy, I knew it was going to be hilarious." My dad was right. It was and still is.

Not many years before my brother's tab troubles, I purchased a rusty Ford Pinto. I am inept at best and disastrous at worst with mechanical things, but my father is an incredible mechanic. After I had the car for a few months, Dad asked me if I had checked the oil lately. I hadn't and in fact was quite mystified as to how to check the oil in that car, thinking that there must be some secret method. So I asked my father, "Dad, how, uh, you know, do I check the oil?" My father, who had vainly tried to educate me in the ways of motors, smiled slightly. "Well, Jack, on that Pinto it's kind of tricky. You need to start the car and then pop the hood and take the cap off the engine top." I smiled, "Yeah, that's what I thought. I was just checking." I should have known something was up when I went out to check the oil because Dad had summoned Mom over and they were watching me from the living room. Of course, that is not the way to check the oil. When I started the car and took the lid off, oil splattered all over me—just as I remembered the right way to check oil. I looked up at the house. My father was laughing so hard he was slapping his leg.

When I was in junior high, my father began to lose his hair, and what he had left turned gray early. I could see he was discomfited by this sign of aging. He was in good shape and considered himself youthful; now his head was betraying him. In jest one day he called himself a geezer. My brother and I laughingly added on that he was an "old geezer." It became a joke in our family and we called him an old geezer with great respect and affection.

Dad returned home on a Monday afternoon after a long weekend conference. My brother and I had missed him badly, so when we saw the car pull up and heard the screen door slam, we ran to the front door, shouting out ahead of us, "Hey, you old geezer, welcome home." Imagine our faces when the person who stood glaring at us just inside the front door was not our father, but a balding, portly man in his late forties, seriously wondering how to teach two loudmouthed boys a lesson. My father had walked in moments after our unorthodox greeting and was nearly overcome by hilarity, although he did his best to salvage the dignity of his pastor friend and traveling companion.

Play and laughter. That is what these stories are about. My dad understood our need for recess and still does his best to bring a sense of play and laughter to his fathering. We laughed loud and long in our family, and I am convinced that our sense of play has held us together during difficult times. I know that my father's intuitive understanding of the need for recess is one of the reasons why I loved him so much when I was a boy. My dad celebrates life and takes everybody near him along for the ride if they will hang on. That has been a tremendous source of strength in our relationship and has been a key building block for many other fathers and sons.

It Isn't Always Easy

Not every father has the same outlook on life as my dad. Some of us are far more serious people. We find it difficult to laugh and play in our relationship with our sons. Many of us feel overwhelmed by the responsibility of fathering a son and we take it all to heart. It is true that life is hard and parenting is sometimes a difficult, thankless task filled with anxiety and unanswered questions. There are rough spots in our lives, and sometimes the rough spots evolve into tragedy. "How," you may ask "am I supposed to build play and laughter into my fathering during a hard life?" The answer is simple. Because life is sometimes nasty and hard, we need to spend time with our sons laughing, playing, and enjoying each other. Another pastor once asked my father how he could make it every day as a counselor, hearing one tragic story after another. Dad replied, "I can handle that stuff because I play hard." When our relationships with our sons is strained, play and laughter will bring us together. When things seem to be slipping away, we need the bond that is formed by sharing a good laugh. When our sons want nothing to do with us, we both need to stop "building a relationship," because that is too hard, and try to simply play together once again as father and son.

There is a memorable scene in the movie *Field of Dreams*. Kevin Costner's character is talking about his father and the strain that existed between them. But then he says, "No matter what happened I could always play catch with my dad. It was our connection. It was what held us together." That character then goes on to tell about how he broke his father's heart by refusing to play catch with him one day; and now years after his father's death this grown man grows quiet and tears spring to his eyes as he wishes for one more chance to play catch with his dad.

Playing together is a remarkable healer of wounds. If your son is young, begin a tradition of playing together right now, because in time this play may be all you have. But it may be enough. It is impossible to overstate the benefits of building playful, laughing times into your relationship.

We bring a scientific grimness to relationships these days. Both our marriage and our parenting relationships have been studied to exhaustion. We know the 300 pitfalls to building a strong family and the many things the experts tell us we must do to make sure disaster doesn't strike our homes. So we put our noses to the grindstone and work at being husbands. We put our heads down and slog it out with our children. Sometimes that may be necessary, but it shouldn't be the way we approach our relationships. We need to look at parenting as a gift from God, a privilege to share our lives with our sons, a great joy to be shapers of our boys. We need recess from the "family is very difficult and unrewarding work" model. We need to add an element of joy into our lives, and I am convinced that play and laughter will take us toward joy and celebration. Without the joy of play and laughter in our relationship, we will have a difficult time making it through the inevitable bumps along the road of life. Mark Twain said, "Against the assault of laughter nothing can stand." Laughter can tear down the walls between you and your son and build a bridge of understanding. Play can be the relentless hammer of love that breaks down the barriers between you and your boy. We invite you to read about two different families and the way play and laughter have helped them as fathers and sons.

Interviewing Dave Claus and his three sons is an adventure. They laugh, they kid each other, and they all talk at the same time. These guys exhibit many of the fathering strengths. They spend a lot of time together. There is terrific spiritual wellness in their family, and they affirm each other often. But what sticks out in my mind about Dave and his sons is that they have a tremendous ability to play and laugh together. Eavesdrop with me for a moment and catch the lively sense of fun that pervades this family:

Question: So what do you do with your dad?
Answers: We play together. We go fishing together.
              Well, I don't do that. I'm not good at fishing.
              That's true.
              We go play sports together.
              Not me, just you.
              Oh, yeah, right.
              We go to movies together. We watch TV.
Question: What TV shows and movies do you watch together?
Answers: "Home Improvement."
              Yeah.
              And *Terminator II.*
              Terminator? In your dreams.
              That's what you hope.
              We also swim together.
              Yeah, and we joke around a lot.
              My dad laughs with me. He's pretty funny.
              I think Dad likes us.
              No he doesn't. He hates us.
              Can you talk about this or not?
              OK, he likes us, but I can't think of what I like about him.
              I want to watch *Terminator II* with him.
              Yeah, in your dreams.
              We spend a lot of time with him.
              I don't. He's at work.
Question: Does your dad work a lot of hours?
Answer: He works about eight hours. . . .

Did you catch all that? That was the unedited conversation we had with Dave and his sons. They are a fun bunch, laughing and stepping on each other's toes and then laughing about that. Dave

Claus has brought a great sense of humor into his relationship with his sons, and it is already paying great dividends.

The Clauses have spent hundreds of hours playing together, and out of that play has come a sense of safety. The Claus boys know their dad will be there for them. Dave coaches his sons' baseball team, not so that he can "straighten them out," but so he can share that part of their life and play more with them. Dave works hard, but he doesn't selfishly guard his time off, protecting his privacy. He lets his kids become a part of his play. Their relationship is being built in the fishing boat, around the TV set, and in the backyard on their hands and knees wrestling. There will be difficult times in the life of the Claus family, but they will make it — in large part because they have created an enormous reservoir of love by playing and laughing together.

Tom and T.C. Cousineau are a different father and son from the Clauses. T.C. is almost finished with high school. His father is the director of a Christian camp in Michigan. Tom and T.C. play together, but they play hard. We caught up to them in Grand Ledge, Michigan where they were rock climbing. We asked them about what made their relationship strong, and although they are far more quiet and more reserved than the Clauses, the answer was the same: they spend a lot of time playing together.

"My earliest memory of my dad is when he was building houses. I remember his work boots would always have tar and stuff stuck on them, and I would sit there and pick that junk off of his boots," T.C. says. "I also remember when we started doing wilderness stuff together in New Hampshire." Tom explains, "He was climbing at Jockey Cap and Artists Bluff at four years old. We've got some great pictures of him up there climbing in the mountains. He did everything young. He was water skiing at three years old. We've always gone off into the woods together, just to be together and have fun together.

"I really enjoy rock climbing. It's kind of a rush for me and T.C. When we climb, we have to have a tremendous amount of trust and confidence in each other. It's not always easy for a father to do with his son, to place my life in his hands. And I do that easily with T.C. I watch him develop, and his technique develop, and I would

71

climb anywhere with him. I would place my life in his hands anywhere on the ropes."

"Its true," T.C. adds. "When you're climbing you have to trust the person. Sometimes when I'm trying a new move, I don't know if I'm going to be able to pull it off. And I'm thinking, *It's OK. If I fall he's there to catch me.* You're willing to try that risky move, you're willing to push yourself because you trust the person on the other end of the rope. I trust my dad."

Tom and T.C. have developed a tremendously strong relationship. They trust and respect each other, they admire each other, they love each other deeply. One of the key ways they have built their relationship is by playing together, climbing mountains, water-skiing, and having fun.

Play, Play, Play

A few months ago I was playing with Jonathon in a big park near our home. We were playing tag and hide-and-go-seek, and he was laughing like crazy because in chasing him I had not noticed a step and had tripped. He knew I wasn't hurt, so we laughed loud and hard about my cartoonish tumble. A woman was watching us intently, and after we had settled down a little bit she approached me and we started to talk. She mentioned that it looked like I was really having fun with my son, and I agreed with her. "Well, enjoy it now, because there will come a time when you won't want to play with him and he won't want to play with you," she said. I smiled and nodded, but afterward I was troubled by her assumption. She assumed that play was for little kids and that when Jay was older we wouldn't share that together. I disagree. I play as much with my dad now, maybe even more now, than I ever did. Play and laughter are not just for fathers with young sons. All of us need recess; all of us need a break from the grind of daily life. Perhaps that need grows as we grow older. I've always believed that recess was wasted on the young. We older types often are in most need of a break. Don't assume that because your son is twenty-five he doesn't want to play with you anymore. It's probably not true. He may need to play with you more than ever.

How to Become a Playful Father

There aren't twelve steps to a carefree and playful life, but there are things that all of us can do to cultivate playfulness and laughter in our relationships with our sons. And they don't depend on personality. Too often we hide behind the fact that we aren't outgoing or extroverted or sports-minded, and we don't use the gifts God has given us. Every father can be a playful father. Every father can bring laughter into the family.

First and foremost, *play for the sake of play.* If you play with an ulterior motive it's not play anymore — it's work. We have too much of that in our parenting already. I don't play video games with my son because it builds our relationship. I do it because it's fun and he beats me and he laughs hysterically when he beats me. Play is not just a means to an end. It is an end in itself. It also is valuable to tell jokes to your son, not to break down walls or facilitate communication, but because it is enjoyable to laugh together. You may protest, "I'm not much of a joke teller." Neither is my dad, and that has never stopped him. In fact, it has at times been a cause for some embarrassment. My father doesn't entirely realize he doesn't tell jokes well, so he tells jokes when he speaks to thousands of people. Then he cannot hear the deafening silence that follows his joke because he is laughing too hard at his own joke. We laugh in our family about my dad's inability to tell a good joke. Humor doesn't take a special personality. If you're not funny, go to funny movies and laugh at funny television shows together.

Do stuff together. Play for no purpose. Go fishing to catch fish, not to talk. Play golf to score, not to "spend quality time together." Play is a worthy expenditure of time in itself, and until we realize that we will not be playful fathers.

Second, *learn to laugh at yourself.* We take ourselves far too seriously and expect others to take us seriously. All of us have our goofy moments. All of us do less-than-intelligent things. Become good at telling stories about your foibles. Ethel Barrymore said, "You grow up the day you have your first real laugh at yourself." Everything is not life-or-death, and your dignity matters only to you. Learn to lighten up and see the little catastrophes that sometimes make up our days for what they are — opportunities to laugh at ourselves. Playfulness begins with us, with seeing the absurd in our lives, with being conscious of irony and nuttiness.

Third, *do things that are completely out of character.* Surprise yourself and your son by occasionally doing something silly. Have an egg fight in the front yard. Get in the tub with the dog when you are giving him a bath. Be weird once in a while. It is freeing and really fun. It will make your son look at you in a new way and give you something to laugh about with him for many years.

Fourth, *program spontaneity.* I know that sounds paradoxical, but it isn't. If you want to be spontaneously fun and playful once in a while, leave room in your schedule and in your budget for that. In other words, prepare to do something on the spur of the moment. Set aside a few dollars in your monthly budget to drive to the nearest big city on the spur of the moment and spend the night in a hotel with an indoor pool. Save time on your calendar so that when a fun idea hits you, you can do it. When I was eight years old, we lived almost four hours away from the rest of my extended family, and we didn't have much money. But one morning as I was getting ready to go to school my father walked into the kitchen and asked my brother and me if we would mind missing two days of school. He and my mother had decided to take two days to visit my grandparents. No reason; they just thought it would be fun. And it was fun, especially to drive past my school on my way to my grandparents' house for an impromptu vacation. Dad had programmed for spontaneity.

Play Makes a Difference

Recess. It needs to be a part of your fathering. We need twelve-minute breaks with our kids. We need to laugh and play with them. If we do we will be happier. We will be able to withstand the difficult times. Playful people are much more prepared for the hardness of life because they have learned to laugh and to find joy in the cracks of life. Henry Ward Beecher said, "A person without a sense of humor is like a wagon without springs, jolted by every pebble in the road." But through humor and play we can build a point of contact with our sons. We can strengthen our relationship, and we can have fun doing it.

Do You Know How to Laugh and Play?

Use the following scale to respond to the following statements:

3 = Often
2 = Sometimes
1 = Seldom

____ 1. I find play in my work.
____ 2. I laugh at myself.
____ 3. I do what I really enjoy doing with my son.
____ 4. I use humor to defuse tense situations.
____ 5. I laugh to reduce stress.
____ 6. I look for humor in stressful family situations.
____ 7. I do not take myself or life too seriously.
____ 8. I see incongruity as funny.
____ 9. I laugh with my son.
____ 10. I read, listen to, or tell humorous stories.
____ 11. I try to laugh at least ten times a day.
____ 12. I "enjoy the moment" with my son.
____ 13. I don't feel guilty about fun times with my son.
____ 14. I don't put off until tomorrow the fun I can have with my son today.
____ 15. I try to expand my leisure and play horizons with my son.
____ 16. I don't rule out an activity with my son because I can't excel.
____ 17. Recess is a priority in my life.
____ 18. I schedule playtimes with my son.
____ 19. I can respond to spontaneous opportunities for play, laughter, and recess with my son.

Scoring: Total your responses.

If you scored 45 or higher you really know how to laugh and play. Keep it up.

A score between 35 and 44 indicates you are doing well. Look for other areas of your life to build more playtime with your son.

A score of less than 35 means you need double recess today! Try to make some adjustments in the way you look at life. Laugh more, smile more, play more, work less, and be more spontaneous.

Recess!

**Some crazy and not-so-crazy ways
to play with your son**

Go skydiving together.

Play hide-and-seek in a large department store.

When you ride an elevator together, turn and face everyone else in the elevator and sing to them.

Starch your son's underwear.

Short sheet his bed.

Go to a concert of his choosing.

Go on a double date with your wife, your son, and his date.

Have a taco-eating contest at the dinner table.

See who can go the longest without changing their socks.

Go to school with your son for a day.

Take your son to work with you for a day.

Play video games with your son.

Let him pick out the videos once in a while.

Build the largest banana split in your town and share it with your son.

Learn to eat Chinese food with chopsticks together.

Learn to sail with your son.

Travel together.

Take a summer and tour every major league baseball park.

Decide together on the ten best rock and roll albums of all time.

Design a dream trip you have always wanted to take and go together.

Play tackle football in the living room.

Get dirty, really dirty.

Cook a gourmet dinner for the rest of the family together.

Volunteer at a local rescue mission or soup kitchen together.

Take a missions trip to the Third World.

Go on a scavenger hunt.

Splatter-paint your son's bedroom together.

Go to a specialty food store and order the strangest stuff they've got. Then go home and dare each other to eat it.

Kiss your teenage son in front of his friends.

77

Chapter Six

An Encouraging Word

...the fathering strength of affirmation and appreciation

By the time I was eighteen years old, I had wrecked three cars. I didn't gently slide them into ditches, or slowly let them deteriorate. I smacked them into other cars with amazing regularity, accompanied by loud crashing sounds and the inevitable sirens. I was a disaster waiting to happen. I never hurt anyone, including myself, but I managed to wreck my father's car twice and my own once before I had graduated from high school.

Most fathers would have torn out their hair, or forbidden me to drive, or at least lost their cool and screamed and yelled a little bit. But not my father. Somehow in midst of the broken glass and tangled metal, he found a way to let me know that no matter what I did on the highways of Michigan, I was still number one in his book. Now that doesn't mean I didn't suffer the consequences for my reckless driving. I paid every insurance deductible and for the increases in my car insurance. Eventually my dad took me shopping for a car of my own to wreck, with the words, "Boy, I think it's time you got yourself a car." My thrill was subdued by the fact that I was paying for that car, and that by helping me purchase a car Dad was ensuring the future of his own car. But I also thought my father was the most incredible dad on earth, because each time I came home with a crinkled fender (or a totaled car), he let me know that he appreciated me. He thought I was wonderful and

79

that he was lucky to have a son like me.

I asked him a few years later why he had responded to my rash of accidents that way. He smiled at me and said, "Jack, I kind of figured that you already knew how stupid you were. I guessed that you had been yelling at yourself long before I came onto the scene, and I figured that at those moments, when you were at your lowest and most vulnerable, you didn't need to hear how badly you had messed up. You needed to know that I thought you were more valuable than any car. You needed to know what was good in you, because you had done a pretty good job of discovering the bad on your own."

The Right Thing

My dad understood intuitively what we have come to learn through our research in later years. Most people have a solid handle on what is wrong with them. If you ask the average teenage boy what is wrong with his life and the way he is living, he can talk for hours. Our sons know what is wrong with them. They tear themselves down over it; they spend hours agonizing over it. What most of us don't know, and what most of our sons don't know, is what is right about them. What is it that makes them special? What is it that makes them a unique gift from the Father God? What is it that you admire about them? What is it that you see in your sons that you really like?

Appreciation and affirmation can turn around your relationship with your son faster than anything else in this book. If you take the time to read the next few pages and to put into practice a simple family appreciation plan, your relationship with your son will grow so fast it might scare you. Even if you and your son are estranged and it seems that nothing can budge the walls that are separating you, appreciation and affirmation have a chance where all else has failed. When we do Parent-Teen Events the first strength we talk about is affirmation and appreciation, because when families practice appreciation so many other issues can be swept away. Strong father-son relationships are built by appreciation and affirmation.

You may be asking, "Why can affirmation make such a difference in my relationship with my son? Why do I need to spend time telling him what's good about him? Won't he get a big head?" The answer to the last question is, "I sure hope so." I hope my son believes every day that I think he is the greatest boy ever put on the earth. I don't want him to act or feel superior to others. I just want him to know that I think he is the greatest, and I want him to know why he is the greatest. When I believe in Jonathon, that frees him to believe in himself. When I believe in Jonathon, that frees him to believe that God believes in him and loves him too. When my son walks out of my home every day with a healthy, realistic, but optimistic view of himself and his possibilities, his chance of striving for the best and doing his utmost to grow as a human being that day are maximized. Simply put, when we affirm and appreciate our sons, they become better human beings. They become more capable of love, less selfish, and more aware of the wonder of this world and of the wonder of God's love for them.

As we interviewed fathers and sons for this book, the fathers' affirmation and appreciation for their sons rang out like a foghorn on a misty evening, telling these sons that they were welcome, appreciated, and loved. Here are a few quick excerpts from some of these interviews:

"The reason I trust him is because Luke is a smart guy. He's got his head screwed on right. He's got it together."

Ed Nienhuis

"His mom and I have always had a lot of confidence in T.C.'s ability to make the right decisions. He has consistently made good choices. He has a good sense about him, and usually he will do the right thing. We trust him, and he's developed and earned that trust."

Tom Cousineau

"My dad was always encouraging me. He would always say, 'You've got to do your best, and I know you can do it. Don't be afraid to try.' "

Dave Claus

"I feel real happy and very proud of David, proud of what I see he's developing into and what he already is, and I'm excited for him and for his future."

Bob Haveman

"Bill is a wonderful young man. He was a wonderful boy. We had a wonderful relationship together. Bill was the boy who always wanted to be with me. I wasn't really all that mechanically minded. Bill only thought so, but we worked very well together."

Harold Roedema

"I knew I was loved by my father more than anything in the world. I can't say I've grown up without faults, but one of the neatest things in my life has been to know that my father loves me more than anything else!"

Tim Vande Guchte

We could fill this book with quotes like these and still not tell the whole story. The fathers we interviewed affirmed and appreciated their sons, and many of them spoke of how they were affirmed by their own fathers. That makes a tremendous difference in a relationship. The finest compliment my father ever paid me was last summer. I was spending time at my parents' cottage with Dad and my son, and about halfway through the weekend Dad took me aside and said, "Jack, I have never seen anyone affirm their child as much as you do with Jonathon. You really build him up." It was the greatest compliment he could pay me, because I want more than almost anything for my children to know that I believe in them, that I think they are the greatest thing on this earth.

I was spending time with a friend of mine who was recently divorced. His life had not been easy of late, and he was nervous about an upcoming visit with his father. He and his dad didn't talk much and didn't like each other a lot, but he was going south to spend some time with him and to let his father spend some time with his two grandkids. I wished him well, and then didn't see or hear from him until about two weeks after he returned from his trip. "How did it go?" I asked him somewhat hesitantly, unsure of

82

the response. As his eyes filled with tears, he smiled and said, "Jack, when I was with my dad, he watched me with my boys. And just before I left for home he grabbed me by the arm and said, 'Son you are a good father. I've been watching you with my grandsons, and you are a fine dad. I'm proud of you.' " My friend looked at me, the tears running freely down his face. "You know what, Jack? In thirty-three years that is the first time my dad ever told me he was proud of me. In thirty-three years that was the first time he let me know that I was doing good. And it felt, well, amazing."

Don't let thirty years pass before you inspire your son with your affirmation and appreciation of him. Purpose in your heart to start right now, whatever the circumstances in your relationship. Do the following exercises, and make affirmation and appreciation a part of your son's life.

Affirmation and appreciation is a threefold process. *First, and perhaps most important, we begin by recognizing positive qualities in our sons.* We need to take the time to see what our sons are doing well. We need to look for areas in which to praise them. Many of us were not raised like this. Our fathers believed that doing right and achieving were to be expected, not to be praised. I can't count the fathers who have told me that their dads never let them know when they were doing well, but were quick to point out their shortcomings and failures. It is time to stop thinking like that. The best way to get our kids to do the right thing is to praise them when they do it. The best way to help them make good choices is to let them know that you see them making good choices and that you believe they can do it. That means we've got to spend the time necessary to recognize positive qualities in our sons.

Take a look at the exercise on the next page, called Accenting the Positive. Too many of us put all of our emphasis on the negatives in our sons. This simple exercise is designed to help us recognize our son's positive qualities. By the way, if your son is junior high age or older, let *him* do this exercise *for you*. One of the most enriching things in life is to be affirmed and appreciated by our sons. It makes our day just as it makes theirs. Make this exercise a family affair, involving everyone. Help each other recognize the positive qualities of each family member.

Accenting the Positive

Write the name of each family member, and then list as many
positive qualities for that person you can think of. Then share your
discoveries with that person. Make a number of copies of this
exercise and do this at least once every couple of weeks. It is simple
but transforming.

Name: Good qualities:

_____

_____

_____

_____

_____

_____

_____

_____

The second aspect of building affirmation and appreciation
builds on the previous exercise. It is not enough to recognize positive qualities in our sons. *We need to express appreciation for those
qualities.* It is OK to think about what fine young men our sons
are, but unless we communicate that to them it isn't doing them
any good. We've got to let our sons know what we think about
them.

I spoke with a forty-six-year-old man recently whose father had just passed away. He was trying to explain to me why he suddenly felt so alone in the world, why he was so depressed, even though he had hardly spoken to his father in ten years. "I guess it's that I never knew what he thought about me. I never knew whether he considered me a success, whether he was glad that he was my father and proud that I was his son. Now I will never know."

Those are not the words I want my son to speak at my passing. Those are not the words I will use when my dad dies. My dad has taken the time to not only recognize positive qualities in me (not an easy task when I was a teenager), but he also has done a great job of communicating that appreciation to me. I know exactly what my father likes about me and why he thinks I'm special. He tells me almost every day.

To help you express appreciation to your son, we have designed an exercise called Just Say It, because so many fathers seem tentative to do just that. In this exercise we've given you the beginning of several sentences. Finish them with words of affirmation and appreciation for your son. Once again, if your son is at least in junior high, do this exercise with him. You will talk about things that will bring you closer in ten minutes than you have been in the last ten months.

Just Say It

Finish the following sentences with only positive comments. Pretend you are speaking to your father/son as you finish the sentence.

I was proud of you when _____

_____

_____

_____

It was special when you _____

_____

_____

_____

The thing I like about you most _____

_____

_____

_____

You are always _____

_____

_____

_____

You are important to me because _____

_____

_____

_____

I think you are amazing when _____

_____

_____

_____

Please make as many copies of this exercise as you need.

The final element of affirmation and appreciation is learning to accept appreciation from others. So many times when we are affirmed by our sons, or wives, or friends we discount it. We refuse to believe it, and our sons do the same thing. We may spend a lot of time expressing our appreciation for them, but it is just water off of a duck's back to them. They aren't listening to us; they are discounting what we are saying. If you feel that is happening with your son, the next time you spend a few minutes telling him why you think he is terrific, don't let him walk away or blow off your comments. Ask him to stop, take a deep breath, and let the reality of your words sink in. Ask him to repeat them to you. Teach him to accept appreciation and let it change his life.

Encouragement: Showing Appreciation

Three principles will help you put this strength to work in your fathering, helping you build a lifelong friendship with your son.

1. Show confidence in your son by letting him know that you trust his abilities. I was in a house last week where the good stereo is off-limits to the teenage sons in the family. The stereo equipment they were allowed to use is older than I am. Their father is a true hi-fidelity guy and thinks it unacceptable for anyone to mess with his stereo. But his teenage boys resent his attitude and feel, rightly, that he doesn't trust them. How encouraging it would be for them if he would let them know why he values his stereo equipment, and how careful he is with it, and then let them use it when he isn't, instructing them in its proper use and holding them accountable, but trusting them and their abilities. That is what is at the heart of appreciation: trusting your son. You and I affirm our sons enormously when we show confidence in their abilities.

2. Build their confidence by acknowledging what they have done well in the past. Keep a scrapbook or journal of everything your son has accomplished, whether major or minor, and bring it out occasionally for him to look at. You don't even have to make a big production about it. Just leave it out, and if he is above the age of six he'll eventually snoop into it. Let him know that you're not keeping a record of his failures, but you do remember what he has done right in the past. This is especially useful when your son is going through a difficult time or has failed in some pursuit. To see his past glories and accomplishments will uplift him and may cause the disappointment of the moment to pass more quickly.

3. Give respect freely by showing your son that he is worth a great deal to you. My dad showed me that I was worth more than any car could ever be by the way he handled my proneness to accidents. I learned that I was much more valuable to him than his possessions. Show your son that you value him. Shower him with affirmation. Rain appreciation on his head. Let him know that nothing you have or could have means more to you than he does.

Jonathon was with my dad not long ago. They were walking around the mall without great purpose or hurry, stopping to look at anything and everything that caught their eye — a time-consuming process when Jonathon's curiosity is piqued. Suddenly, Jonathon grabbed his grandpa's hand and looked at him. "You just like to be with me, don't you, Grandpa? You just think I'm cool." "Yeah, Jonathon, that is exactly right," my dad replied.

Our prayer for you is that your son will grab your hand and utter the same words, and that by expressing appreciation and by affirming your son, you will make your relationship richer, deeper, and stronger.

Family Appreciation Plan

1. Set aside a certain time at least once a week that will be free from distractions.

2. Share positive thoughts, feelings, and desires with your son. Be honest and vulnerable.

3. Use language that expresses appreciation. For instance, "I appreciate it when you. . . ."

An Encouraging Word

64 Ways to Say, "Very Good"

Families thrive in a climate of love, so give your family members warmth and physical signs of affection. Look for good behaviors and attitudes you want to strengthen, and then say, "VERY GOOD" in a variety of ways. Here are some suggestions:

I'm proud of you.
You're doing a good job.
Congratulations.
I knew you could do it.
Now you're cookin'.
GREAT!
Good for you.
You make it look easy.
Not bad.
You're learning fast.
Couldn't have done it better myself.
That's quite an improvement.
Now you have it.
Nice try!
That's the way to do it!
WOW!
Keep up the good work.
That's better.
SENSATIONAL!
You are amazing.
I'm so glad you are mine.
You did that very well.
I can't believe it!
FANTASTIC!
Nothing can stop you now.
TREMENDOUS!
Good thinking.
Keep on trying.
I like that.
You're right on target.
That's it.
WAY TO GO!

MARVELOUS!
You have got it made.
That's GOOD.
STUNNING!
You're doing beautifully.
You outdid yourself.
Absolutely WONDERFUL!
SUPERB!
It is fun just being with you.
I wouldn't trade you for the world.
You are the BEST!
I can't stop thinking about you.
I love you.
You are my friend.
You are so thoughtful.
You do such a good job.
You're right.
Clever.
EXCELLENT!
What a great person you are.
PERFECT!
I think you are so kind.
I'm always proud to be with you.
I couldn't wish for someone better.
You've got that down pat.
Nobody does it better.
You did well today.
WELL DONE!
What a job!
Great work.
You did it that time.
Good idea.

Everything Changes

...the fathering strength of adaptability

*Phil Cok is thirty-eight years old and a partner in a communica-
tions and advertising firm. He's been in advertising for the better
part of a decade. Phil is down-to-earth, with a quick smile and a
ready laugh. His son, Mitchell, is sixteen years old, a serious
student, and a serious Christian. Mitchell has a self-deprecating
sense of humor and a transparent honesty. If Mitchell believes in
something, he really goes for it. Together they spend a lot of time
hunting and fishing, but they don't usually catch anything.
"That's pretty much been our story. We fish and come home without fish. We hunt and see nothing but trees," Phil says.*

*Harold and Troy Isenhoff are go-getters. Both of them have started
their own businesses, and forty-four-year-old Harold lists inline
skating among his many hobbies. With a college degree in business
management you might expect his twenty-two-year-old son Troy
to follow in his footsteps. But Troy has followed his own dreams,
starting a business while still in college, a business that now
demands his full-time attention.*

What do you do if you're not necessarily a great outdoors kind
of guy and your teenage son is absolutely nuts about hunting,
fishing, hiking, and camping? What do you do when your interests

run to other things, but your son won't do those things with you because he is absorbed in his own world? What do you do if spending a week in a tent in the snow sounds like torture to you and like heaven to your teenage son?

If you're Phil Cok, you pack wool socks and an extra pair of long underwear, ruefully wave good-bye to your wife and daughters, and go hunting with your son. "It was what Mitchell wanted to do. If I wanted to be with him, and I did, then I was going to have to change a little bit and do some things that Mitchell wanted to do," Phil says. Mitch remembers his dad. "It's 6 in the morning, the sun isn't even up yet, and Dad is lying down in the deer blind, wrapped in a blanket, just about freezing to death." "Yeah," says Phil, "I remember that. I'm sitting in my blind with my camera; you're in another blind with your bow. And of course we didn't see anything." Phil and Mitch look across the table at each other, and a smile crosses both of their faces. The affection they share for each other is obvious and infectious. These two guys like each other and like telling stories about their time together. As their relationship has required changes, they have been able to make those changes and have strengthened their friendship and their love for each other in the process.

Adaptability is a key fathering strength. It is vital as our sons grow and mature that our relationship grows and matures as well. It is vital as the environment in which we father changes that our relationship changes to keep pace with it. This trait is called *adaptability*. In other words, adaptability means striking the right balance between changing when it is needed and good for the relationship and creating an atmosphere of stability that builds a relationship.

It is key that we become adaptable fathers and that our families learn the strength of adaptability. If we don't, a promising relationship can turn sour in a hurry. Rick was sitting in my office wondering what had gone wrong in his family. He is an eighteen-year-old boy who truly loves his parents and wants the best for his family. But he and his father have been at war for almost two years. Rick remembers "sitting on my dad's lap at University of Michigan football games. My dad is a Michigan alum and has great season tickets to Michigan football. I remember sitting with him, singing the Michigan fight song, cheering our lungs out for the maize and blue. I thought he was the greatest guy in the world. Well, I don't necessarily feel that way now."

What happened? What changed in the intervening years? "I grew up and I guess my dad didn't want that to happen," Rick says. "I think he still wants me to be that little boy on his lap at the Michigan game. But I'm not that boy anymore. I'm a man, but I'm still treated like a child."

"What is it that you want from your dad, Rick? What do you need?"

"I need him to realize that we need to 'grow up' the way we talk to each other. We need to change the way we relate. I'm not going to listen and nod my head. I've got ideas too."

Rick and his dad started out right: they spent time together, and they showed love and appreciation for one another. Their family has strong values and morals that have been clearly communicated. But their relationship is not adaptable. It has remained in the same place for many years, rigid and unmoving, which has caused Rick and his father to lose sight of each other. Their relationship has run aground because they didn't know how to adapt when change was called for.

Rob wonders why his grown son is so emotionally distant from him. Once upon a time they were connected, they were friends. But since Rob's divorce they are having a tough time. Even though Rob sees his son nearly as much as he always did, the divorce, even though it was as amicable as divorces can be, has put a wall between them, and Rob doesn't know what to do. He is afraid that his twenty-five-year-old son is slipping away just when Rob was really beginning to enjoy him.

Rob's problem is the same as Rick's. They both need to adapt to a changing environment. Rob's relationship with his son has got to change to deal with the new reality of divorce. If Rob wants it to be the same as it always was, he's going to struggle because it can't be the same. The milieu that produced that relationship no longer exists, so the relationship must change with the environment and adapt to the new realities, or it will die.

In this chapter we will examine this fathering strength of adaptability. We also will answer some key questions by looking at our life and at the lives of two sets of fathers and sons who have done a great job of adapting when it was needed. The key question we need to answer is, How can our father-son relationship change with a changing environment without losing its identity?

To answer that question we need to answer three related questions:

1. *What changes are required as your son grows up, moving through the stages of childhood, adolescence, and adulthood?*

2. *How does a father continue to grow his relationship with his son when his son pursues different dreams?*

3. *How does the changing family environment (job change or loss, relocation, death, or divorce) affect our father-son relationship?*

My father is not by nature a compromising person. It is in his nature and makeup to do what he wants and to get what he wants. He is usually very sure of his position. I remember a couple of revealing, though definitely tongue-in-cheek sayings he used to tell my brother and me. My favorite was, "Those of you who think you are perfect are annoying to those of us who are." My brother's favorite was when after he would accuse my father of being mistaken, my dad would invariably say, "I was wrong once — that was when I thought I was wrong and found out later that I really wasn't." Funny stuff, especially when my father said it with a big smile on his face and a goofy laugh. But there was also a hint of truth in those words. My father is not naturally a yielding man.

Dad and I spent most of my childhood discovering that in a battle of wills we had each met our match. Although as the father he had the upper hand, I was probably as unyielding as he was. Our relationship could have foundered during my adolescence, when I became the poster child for the "nut-brained philosophy of the month club." I came home and said a lot of things designed to irritate my parents, things I knew would grate especially on my straight-arrow, conservative, Republican pastor-father. If he had been the same man when I was sixteen that he had been when I was six, you would not be reading this book today, because his rigidity and uncompromising attitude would have driven me away. But my dad realized that what had worked at six wouldn't necessarily work at sixteen. He realized that as I grew he would have to grow as well, and that the only way our relationship (a relationship of two strong-willed and opinionated people) would survive was if our relationship grew with both of us. So he made sure that it did grow, and he made sure that he grew. And as he grew I knew, watching him, what I wanted to be. I wanted to be like him.

We fought our battles during high school, but Dad, even though I'm sure it was difficult for him, knew he had to relax. He couldn't challenge every dumb thing I said. He needed to give me room to explore, and he needed to become more compromising. That is adaptability, and if my dad could learn it, then so can you and I.

Phil and Mitch Cok's relationship, mentioned at the beginning of this chapter, is a terrific example of adaptability at work in a small way that has brought great rewards and growth to their friendship. Mitch realizes that his dad didn't have to change, that he could have let Mitch go off into the woods with his friends. But Phil saw this as an opportunity to build their relationship. And he also realized that if he didn't change, his son would grow away from him. "My dad spent that time with me, hunting and fishing, because he cared about me," Mitch says. "He wanted to be with me. He wanted to do stuff with me. I think his dad worked so much that he didn't want that to happen with us. He wanted our relationship to be different."

Mitch's comment brings up an interesting point. Not only was Phil adaptable by acquiring an interest in the things that interested his son, he also adapted by changing his fathering style from the model he had grown up with. Phil talks with affection about his own father, and it's obvious they loved each other. But he also talks about the time they didn't have, about the relationship that could have been. Phil has determined that he will make the changes necessary in his life and his fathering to keep growing his relationship with his son. "There was nothing else Mitch wanted to do for about three years," Phil says. "He was really obsessed with this outdoors thing. I probably would have done some fishing on my own accord, but it was all that Mitch read about or talked about. My dad had a hardware store and worked all the time. I can remember three times that we went out hunting together. I didn't want that for us. So when Mitch got interested and stayed interested, I got interested too. I had to."

Developmental Changes

It is much easier to be adaptable if our fathers exhibited this strength in their lives. Adaptability comes easily for some fathers. Many times they are fathers who had adaptable fathers. For the rest of us, being adaptable will take some work and close attention. The tough thing about fathering is that just when you think you've got it down pat, your son moves into another developmental stage and it seems like you are back to square one. That is why this characteristic is so important. If we want to be consistently good fathers, from wherever we are starting, we need to be flexible, changing the relationship as the environment and needs of that relationship change.

Right now my son, Jonathon, is five years old. Every time I put my coat on he runs and gets his too. He wants to go everywhere with me and thinks he is being cheated of something if he has to stay home or go to something of little importance, like school. Being with me is the highlight of his life, but it will not always be that way. As he grows up he will change his feelings about being with me. It will no longer be the highlight of his life. In fact, as much as it pains me to think about it, when he enters junior high and especially high school, I may become a point of embarrassment to him. Right now he'll do anything with me; my agenda rules. In ten years if I want to spend time with him, I will have to follow his agenda. He will set at least some of the rules.

That is why Phil Cok decided to take up hunting. His son wanted to hunt, and that was the best opportunity to be with him. So he changed his interests to his son's and followed his son's agenda. As our sons grow and mature, their interests will change, and if our relationship doesn't change, at least some of the time, we run the risk of losing contact.

There are at least four ways that our relationship will have to change as our children move through the developmental stages:

Baby to Buddy (birth to 6)
Buddy to Teacher (6 to 12)
Teacher to Cheerleader (12 to 17)
Cheerleader to Peer (17 to 25)

Baby to Buddy

The first stage of our relationship with our son is *baby to buddy*. During this early stage our children need our presence, our affection, and our unconditional love. This is when it is fun to be a dad because your son is convinced that the world revolves around you. We are their heroes, what they want to be when they grow up. I asked Jonathon what he wants to be when he grows up. He said he wants to be a golfer (I play golf badly, but my son thinks I'm Jack Nicklaus), a writer, a speaker, a pastor, and a cowboy. I was puffed up with pride, for most of those things are reflections of me. My son wants to be me when he grows up. I was feeling quite pleased with myself when my wife gently burst my bubble. "Ask him the same question in ten years, Jack. I bet he doesn't answer the same." Then she smiled and walked away, knowing that at fifteen things will most assuredly be different for Jonathon.

If we settle into the buddy role that is necessary from birth to early childhood too comfortably, we will miss what is to come next. And like many fathers we will continue to treat our sons and our relationship with the same tone and the same buddy-buddy attitude long after they have moved out of that stage. That is where tension and difficulty can invade our fathering. We wonder what happened. We wonder why the things that brought us close together at age five don't work at ten, or twelve, or fifteen. If we want to continue to build beyond early childhood, we need to change our relationship.

Buddy to Teacher

The second stage is *buddy to teacher*. As our children move out of
early childhood, sometime between ages six and eight, they need a
teacher, a father who can help them learn. At this age kids are
searching—some of them desperately—for competency. They
want to be good at something. A father of an eleven-year-old boy
told me of a conversation he had with his son. His son was a lousy
kickball player, and kickball was the sport of choice at his school
during recess. The father told his son, "Don't worry, everybody is
good at something. You don't have to be the best kickball player in
the world. You will be good at something else." The boy looked up
at him, "But, Dad, I'm not good at anything." And he began to
cry. That father held his boy in his arms and determined to teach
his son how to do something well.

The father had been a great sailor but had sold his boat when
he got married and had kids. So he and his son went and picked
out an old sailboat, strapped it to the top of their car, and learned
to sail. That eleven-year-old spent almost every spare minute
learning about sailing that summer, and when he returned to
school he had a new confidence. When he was passed over as
teams were picked for kickball he didn't mind as much, because he
knew that he could sail his boat all by himself. He knew that when
the wind kicked up and the waves crested he was in his element
and could handle it. And kickball seemed a small thing in compari-
son. This boy knew something else. He knew that his father cared
about him and loved him. He knew that his dad had taken the
time to teach him something, and his relationship with his father
grew through that experience.

As teachers we can pass on the skills we have acquired over a
lifetime. What we teach doesn't have to be as arcane as sailing; it
can be simple stuff. My father taught my brother how to fix things.
He taught me how to water-ski. He taught my brother how to
build. He taught me to drive a tractor. These were not landmark
events in and of themselves, but as a whole they were a remarkably effective means of building our friendship. It would not have
been possible had my dad been unwilling or unable to move out of

the buddy role that he was so good at and redefine his fathering as a teacher.

Much of our teaching can be done informally, through modeling what we know. Kids like to learn from watching instead of by a strict lesson approach. All of this teaching must be done with an eye toward the unique interests of our sons. A common pitfall when taking on the role of teacher is to assume that your kids like everything that you like. Remember, they are moving beyond that stage in their lives. They are beginning to assert themselves, to discover their talents, interests, and gifts. It is counterproductive for us to push them into our interests. It may be necessary for you to learn a new skill that interests your son and then to pass it along to him or even to learn with him.

Proverbs 22:6 is a much quoted and often ill-used verse. It says, "Train a child in the way he should go, and when he is old he will not turn from it." This verse does not guarantee that if we do the right things as parents our kids will turn out right. Instead, it points toward the unique gifts and abilities of our sons and tells us that by training them to use those God-given gifts and following up on those interests, our children will build good habits and skills that will last a lifetime. It is our job as our sons' teachers to help them discover their gifts and to encourage them to fly.

Our adaptability can be crucial to our children in the middle years of childhood. By changing our relationship to that of teacher and by becoming sensitive to our sons' interests and talents, we can help them become the people God wants them to be. We can, in the words of author Thom Black, "help them soar" (*Born to Fly*, Zondervan, 1994). The key is to become adaptable, changing the relationship to fit our sons' changing needs.

Teacher to Cheerleader

Up to this point most of us do rather well, but this next transition, from *teacher to cheerleader*, is difficult for many fathers. When we were buddies and teachers we had the upper hand. Lines of authority were clearly defined. In fact, being a good father usually resulted in a boosted self-esteem and our children regarding us with a measure of awe or, at the very least, respect. When our children begin to move into adolescence, they need us to become their cheerleaders. They need us to adapt by giving up a measure of control.

That is incredibly difficult, because during this time we feel the need for the most control. During this time we feel the most fear, and that fear often moves us to clamp down on our sons, denying them the freedom and the responsibility they both crave and require. Perhaps that is why good father-son relationships can be wrecked so easily during adolescence.

To understand the way we need to adapt at this stage of our sons' lives, we need to understand what is happening with them during this time. The developmental task for our sons during adolescence is formation of identity. That means during this period they need to figure out who they are apart from us, their fathers. They need to build a sense of self that will carry them through adolescence and into adulthood. To do that they need some space. They need to be able to try on different identities without recrimination. They need fathers who treat them as unique individuals, cheering them on as they move into adulthood. In moving from teacher to cheerleader, we need to find ways to help our sons figure out who they are without interfering in that process. We cannot build their identity for them; they must do it themselves. But we can assist them. Fathering during adolescence demands a balancing act between too much involvement and too little direction. It means that we have to let our sons fail and learn the consequences of their failures.

Perhaps the best thing we can do for them during this stage is to become their unflagging cheerleader. Our teenage sons need someone to believe in them, to give them the rock-solid support that is necessary to begin the scary process of building identity. If they know that we believe in them and have faith in them and are always on the sidelines cheering for them, they will feel the freedom to become what God wants them to become. They will know that even when they fail we will not give up on them but will help dust them off and send them back into the game.

Now please don't misunderstand. We are not advocating a

cheerful acceptance of everything your son does, right or wrong. We believe that careful limits, appropriate to their age, enhance freedom and add to identity. We are not saying that everything your son does should meet with your unqualified acceptance. The high-wire act of parenting a teenage son requires careful balancing and a deft touch. We need to give responsibility and let our children learn what that means. Sometimes that means allowing them to fail and suffer the consequences. But we can always be their cheerleader. We can always believe in them.

The crucial difference in this stage of life is that our sons no longer need us on the playing field with them. In fact, they need us to stop blocking for them, to stop running interference and clearing the obstacles out of their path. They need to experience life on its own terms, with all of its difficulties and joys, as they figure out who and what they want to be. Our job is to move to the sidelines and cheer them all the way.

Cheerleader to Peer

The most important adaptation we need to make is from *cheerleader to peer*. As they grow into adulthood, our sons need us to treat them as adults. They no longer need us to stand on the sidelines and cheer them along; they need us to welcome them into the company of men, to accept them as adults, our equals. One friend told me once that you are never a real man until your father dies, because until then you are always a son. I believe he is wrong. But too often his point is right: that no matter what our sons accomplish we still treat them as sons, loved maybe, certainly with pride, but with an element of condescension.

I once read about a pro football quarterback who, after leading his team to the playoffs and becoming one of the highest paid men on his team, would go home during the off-season and stay with his mom and dad in the same room he grew up in. The article on this quarterback showed a picture of his room. It was the room of a typical fifteen-year-old boy: sports posters lining the walls, dirty socks and underwear strewn on the floor. The story lauded the player for his "down-to-earth" love for his parents but went on to

101

say that the only criticism his teammates had was that when the pressure built in a game, he sometimes folded and made bad choices, often resulting in an interception or a sack.

This quarterback's decision-making skills will not improve soon. He is still a child, and his father treats him as such. He has never learned adult responsibility. Many of us do the same things with our sons. We do not treat them as peers, even when they have proven that they are men and no longer boys. We must adapt our relationship and begin to treat them as equals.

What does that mean? It means we value their opinions as we value the opinions and beliefs of other adults. It means we ask advice occasionally, that we are no longer "the answer-man." It means treating them as friends, with all the privileges and responsibilities inherent in that relationship. It means valuing their ideas, hopes, and dreams. In our family this happened because my father willingly gave up the role of teacher, cheerleader, and buddy. He treated his two sons as equals, and we have become men because of that treatment. I still call my father for advice on many things, from marriage to lawn mowers. But a typical day is just as likely to see him calling me because his computer is acting strangely and he needs help, or because a sermon isn't coming together and he needs a couple of ideas. Every time he asks me for help I feel privileged and proud, because I know my father believes I am his equal, his peer. And that gives me confidence that influences the rest of my life.

One other word about this final adaptation. Much of what passes for manhood in this culture is bluster and bravado. Whether it is the image of a big-screen tough guy mouthing off to the bad guys before he mows them down with his machine gun, or the man as an island, needing neither affection nor acceptance, this image of men has influenced us enormously. One of the reasons we gravitate to those models of manhood is because many fathers haven't given their sons permission to be men on their own terms. They haven't grown up their relationship. They still treat their sons as children. If we treat our sons as men, they will not have to look to Hollywood for that model. They will see a model of manhood in us, and they will be comfortable with their own manliness because we have treated them as men. They won't have anything to prove to anybody.

Your Dreams, His Dreams

Harold Isenhoff would love for his son to go to college, to get his degree, and then to get a good job. That is, after all, what most of us want for our kids. We all have dreams for our sons, and usually those dreams include an education and a well-paid career. Harold's son, Troy, is a smart, motivated twenty-two-year-old who had different dreams for his life. And what makes Harold and Troy's relationship special is the way they have adapted their relationship to fit Troy's hopes and dreams. Harold has done something that is difficult for many fathers. He has stopped pushing his son to do what he, Harold, wants him to do with his life and instead has set about helping Troy achieve his own dreams.

Right now Troy is back in school, part-time, but his main job is to run the lawn service business he started with a friend when he was nineteen. Harold talks about the time when he realized his son didn't want to go to college but wanted to go into business for himself: "I knew it was going to interfere with school and with a few things in life. It's not the normal track you see a lot of kids take. But the experience, and the education, and the benefits will be irreplaceable. We're not disappointed about that. We want him to do what he wants to do, so I helped him start up this business about three years ago."

"My dad has always been supportive," Troy adds gratefully. "Some fathers . . . well, it seems that it's all about what they want, and they don't care much about their kids. My dad's not like that. He's been supportive of me in everything I do."

"The thing I admire most about Troy is that he is an independent thinker. He is able to be a self-starter. I never had to push him," says Harold. "Maybe his goals have changed a couple of times, but that doesn't concern me. He is going to do well."

As you read Harold's and Troy's words, one thing quickly becomes apparent. Theirs is an adaptable relationship. Harold has been able to let Troy become what he wants to become. He hasn't been so wrapped up in his dreams for his son that he forgot about his son's desires. And this adaptability has helped their relationship flourish and grow. The freedom to choose his own path has made Troy Isenhoff an outstanding person, self-reliant and goal-oriented. If his father had been breathing down his neck with questions about school, work, and career, he wouldn't be where he is today, nor would their relationship be where it is today.

Through their example we can learn three simple things about letting our sons' dreams become our dreams. First, *our kids need the freedom to dream.* If we spend all of our time communicating our dreams to them, they won't be able to formulate their own dreams. They must be encouraged to dream big dreams for their lives and to strive to reach those dreams.

Second, *our support is crucial in the early stages of their dreams.* Harold helped Troy begin his business. He gave him the emotional support that enabled Troy to risk and take a chance on achieving his dream. He probably couldn't have done it without the support of his father. Many fathers underestimate the importance of their moral support, their power to encourage their sons. When our sons begin to chase their dreams, they need us to cheer them on.

Finally, *our sons need us to believe in them and have faith in them.* They need to know we are in their corner, that we believe they are terrific, and capable, and can achieve their hopes and dreams for their lives. Without the foundation of our belief in them, they will have a difficult time building their lives and pursuing their dreams.

Coping with a Changing Family Environment

Earlier in this chapter you met Rob, a divorced father of a grown son who is struggling to adapt his relationship to fit the changing family environment. You read about his growing estrangement from his son and his frustration with that. Rob is not alone. Many fathers struggle enormously with adapting their relationship as the family changes. Divorce, job loss, relocation, death, or serious family illness place enormous demands on the father-son relationship. During these times all the hard work of many years of relationship-building can come crashing down. Divorce, with its complicated loyalties, anger, betrayal, and disappointment, can spell the end of a good father-son friendship. Losing your job, with all of the shame that sometimes accompanies that event, or the relocation of the family, can stress an already-fragile relationship. How can you and I build the strength of adaptability into our lives during this time and survive, maybe even thrive?

1. Acknowledge that it is OK to be different. Some of us have a hard time accepting differences in other people. We also have a difficult time adjusting to differences in our own lives. When our changing environment demands that we change, maybe to something we don't want to be (for instance, single instead of married), we need to acknowledge that different is OK. It is not a curse. Without acknowledging that fact, we will find it impossible to adapt our relationship and we'll struggle. One friend put it well: "I can accept the fact that divorce happens to people. I can even talk about God's forgiveness and love for divorced people. But I never thought I would get divorced. It's much easier to handle other people's differences and much harder to deal with my own." This friend was adapting as a father following a messy divorce, and being a single parent was killing him. Even the term "single parent" was enough to drive him crazy. He had to recognize that being a single father was reality now, and though it wasn't the best option it was better than being an absentee father. He had to acknowledge the difference in his life and in his relationship with his son and adapt to that change.

2. Appreciate the opportunity to grow. We run the risk of sounding trite by suggesting this, but this time in your life has great potential for growth. One father, a high-level executive replaced during a corporate takeover, expressed this idea admirably. "I have been thinking recently that we needed to live more simply. I wondered if I would still be a serious follower of Jesus if my life had taken a decidedly poorer turn. Well, now we get to find out. And we get to find out if everything I've been telling my son about God's provision is what I really believe."

Adapting to change can be terrifically stretching. We can become better people, better fathers, and better followers of Jesus through adapting to difficult times. Don't look upon the need to change as a curse. Try to reframe it and see it as a chance to grow, a chance to let God make you into someone more honest and real.

3. Accept one another as unique creations of God. Adapting is ultimately about acceptance. We give up our ideals and our ideas of what a perfect family or relationship will look like and work like, and we accept our children, our wives, our situations just as they are presented to us. Adapting will become much easier when we are able to look at differences in others as facets of God's marvelous creation instead of as mistakes that we were put on earth to fix. We will learn to adapt and build a much stronger relationship with our sons if we can learn to accept our situations, no matter how bleak, as part of God's working in our lives.

The bottom line is that adaptability is a must if we are to develop a lifelong friendship with our sons. Our relationship may flourish and grow for a short time without our adapting, but it will wither on the vine if we do not water it and fertilize with adaptation. Strong fathers and sons are not afraid to change their relationship when it is needed. They balance that change by holding on to some things for dear life — things like love, respect, affirmation, and trust. But as the environment changes, and as your son changes, it will be necessary to adapt to meet the changing needs of the relationship. If we don't change when it is needed, we will never enjoy the rich fullness of a lifelong friendship with our sons.

*How Adaptable Are You?**

Complete the following checklist using the response choices below:

    1 = Almost never
    2 = Once in a while
    3 = Sometimes
    4 = Frequently
    5 = Almost always

Everything Changes

Describe your family as you see them now:

___ 1. Different persons act as leaders in my family.
___ 2. My family changes its way of handling tasks.
___ 3. I am willing to change my interests and hobbies to fit my son's changing interests and hobbies.
___ 4. Household responsibilities shift from person to person in my family.
___ 5. My son and I try new ways of dealing with problems.
___ 6. We make decisions together in my family.
___ 7. We are flexible in handling our differences.
___ 8. We compromise when resolving problems.
___ 9. My son and I are changing the way we relate to each other as we grow up together.
___ 10. Rules change in our family.

Scoring: Total your responses.
If you scored below 19, you may need to loosen up a bit and work on becoming more adaptable.
If you scored between 19 and 24, you are fairly structured but able to adapt when it is demanded.
If you scored between 24 and 28, you are quite flexible, share leadership, and are able to adapt when necessary.
A score above 28 may indicate too much change in your family. You might need to work on more consistency and structure.

*Adapted from Circumplex Model of Marital and Family Systems, Dr. David Olson, University of Minnesota. Used by permission.

Chapter Eight

More Than Words Can Say

...the fathering strength of communication

Gary DeGraaf is a plant manager for a company that supplies the auto industry. His sons, Derek, nineteen, and an engineering student, and Aaron, eighteen, a high school student, recall that their father was a stern, hard-to-please man. But that aspect of their life together was tempered by a terrific, open communication that made them feel valued and respected.

Paul Hillman is a thoughtful, reflective, forty-seven-year-old partner in an editing firm. His son Nathan is a senior at the University of Wisconsin. They share a love of words and learning that binds them together even now, when they communicate mostly via e-mail.

It was not a pretty sight. Not for the squeamish or the faint-hearted; certainly not for the easily offended. No, this is not the opening line to a bad mystery novel. Rather, I am describing a typical dinner at the Schreur household when I was in high school and college. It was a loud and fairly raucous event. I had no idea until I was in college that some people ate silently and spoke only when it was absolutely necessary at dinner. I had no idea that for some people the dinner hour was about relaxation and quiet contemplation. Dinner at my house was a free-for-all.

Conversation often would begin with an acerbic comment on

the news of the day by me or my father, followed by a disagreement on that comment, a heated discussion about the point, and then — as the argument degenerated into the absurd — a joke that finished off the conversation. The dinner table was our bully pulpit, and everyone was welcome to state his or her opinions. But everybody's opinion was not respected. Opinions that were ventured without rationality and without at least the modicum of an argument were torn down and thrown back to the poor soul foolish enough to venture such a lousy idea. Perhaps I am overstating it a bit, but the truth is that we communicated over dinner, and it had nothing to do with how old we were or what our life experience was. Our dinner table arguments were all about logic, reason, and certainly passion. It was fun and good training, but most of all it built me up.

How is a person built up by having to defend his ideas and opinions? The answer is hard to explain, but I'll try. I knew growing up that my dad respected my opinions and my ability to reason so much that he was willing to argue with me. I'm not talking about angry words or disrespect. We argued points. We agreed and disagreed. We discussed the merits and logic of almost everything under the sun, and I knew that my dad was listening to me and that he cared about what I had to say. It may not be conventional, but it was how we communicated and it worked. And somehow through those full-family dinner table discussions I learned what it meant to be a son, and by watching my dad I knew that I was loved.

Don't Skip This Chapter Yet. Read This First!

My guess is that you were tempted to skip this chapter when you saw the subtitle. You are probably a little tired of hearing about communication. Frankly, so am I. Too often when family "experts" speak about communication it either becomes a very "touchy-feely" thing that is really more dependent on personality than anything else, or it becomes a dry and boring discussion of the levels of communication and the ways we communicate. You probably know most of that stuff, and what you don't know isn't

110

all that important. In this chapter we won't talk about how to communicate with your son. For one thing, that could very well be an entire book; and in fact, whole books have been written on the subject. Second, we don't believe that there is a "right" way to communicate. All of us have different communication styles and that is OK. Some people are loud, talkative, and blunt. Others communicate quietly through their attitudes and expressions more than by their words. It doesn't matter what your communication style is, as long as the goal of communication is accomplished. Communication is simply all of the ways that we transmit information from one person to another, and the reason we do that is to achieve understanding. In other words, as long as the message sent is equal to the message received, communication is taking place, and understanding is occurring. Positive communication, which should be our goal, accomplishes understanding while building each other up, not tearing each other down.

In this chapter we want to show you how two families, neither of them a touchy-feely family, have enriched their life with good communication. We'll show you how the key for these fathers and sons has been communication. And then we will talk about how communication is essential to overcoming the difficulties involved in fathering sons in the nineties. So stay with us as we discover that communication is more than words can say.

Gary DeGraaf is a demanding father. He is stern, and in all honesty he probably expected more of his two sons than he should have. He is a perfectionist, a strong disciplinarian. He is not your prototypical "soft, nineties" guy. He is a good man, but a tough one. Yet his relationship with his two sons is nothing short of extraordinary. Instead of rebelling against his discipline, his sons thrived under it, even when they didn't like it, and their relationship thrived as well. The reason they have the relationship they now enjoy is because of one thing: communication.

"In raising my boys I tried to use the examples of my childhood, the good and the bad," Gary says. "I was strong on accountability with all of my children. There were consequences for wrong actions. The emphasis was not on rigid rules, but points of view on an issue. It was really about communication. I tried to talk about

111

everything with my sons, without exception; everything was open for discussion. So we talked a lot about values, about why I believed the way I did, about the thought processes that should be going on before decisions are made. And the emphasis on communication is working. It is still a focal point today. They bring friends over and we get into wide-ranging discussions. And even their friends get involved in the communication."

Gary knew that he had to balance his strong, disciplinarian approach to fathering with communication so that his kids would always have an avenue to discuss with him what was going on in their lives. Even though he was a strict father, they weren't afraid of him because he listened to them, and they understood each other. Communication was the balance in their family. His sons had to obey him, but it wasn't a mindless obedience. They also were free to challenge his ideas and to talk those things out.

"My wife and I challenged them to think, to always bring another point of view — not just their parents' — to the discussion," Gary says. "We shared what our view was and then said, 'Now here is how some other people view this,' so that our kids didn't just grow up on our dogma."

Derek DeGraaf echoed his father's statements and added that there was a lot of humor in the communication, and that made the tough medicine of discipline easier to swallow. "Humor has been a big deal in our family. It's an ongoing thing — an inside joke here, an inside joke there. I feel comfortable talking with my dad. He listens. Ever since I can remember we've been able to talk about things. He's pretty strict, you know, a tough guy about discipline. He always has been there to talk to. If there's something going on he'll take us aside, maybe individually. Sometimes we'll have a family talk after dinner."

Good father-son communication is often built on a pattern, a set way of dealing with difficult issues, rituals that help ease everyone into the communication. That is certainly the case in the DeGraaf family. "You know Dad's going to say something, because after dinner he kind of leans back in his chair and clears his throat, and then the family talk begins," Derek says. "It's easy to talk to my dad because he listens to the entire situation. If he hears something he's not one-sided. He listens, and he's very patient when he listens."

Communication as a Navigation Aid

Gary, Aaron, and Derek DeGraaf have a special relationship. They have been able to maintain that relationship in an atmosphere of high expectations and tough discipline, because they found out how to communicate with each other and then spent time doing it. Gary took the time to listen to his sons, to hear about the world from their point of view, to take their values and beliefs seriously. Communication will help you and me keep our relationship with our sons growing as well by helping us navigate some difficult waters. The rapids that all of us will face as we father our sons include:

1. *Discipline*

2. *Expectations*

3. *Failure*

4. *Values*

5. *Dreams*

If we utilize the fathering strength of communication, we will be able to navigate through those difficult waters, coming out on the other side not merely as survivors, but stronger and closer to our sons.

Discipline

I don't think my dad was a tough disciplinarian by his standards, but certainly by the standards of today he was. I was spanked as often as any child, and probably deserved most of those spankings. But I never got angry with my father for spanking me. I never

wondered if he had the right to inflict his discipline on me, because when he disciplined me I knew what it was for. I knew what I had done wrong, and I knew the rule I had broken. Discipline worked in my family because it was always accompanied by good communication. And that didn't stop when the spankings stopped. When I was in high school and was grounded I knew why, and I understood the need to be punished. I didn't like it, and I'm sure I protested strongly and loudly. But my dad's discipline worked on me as an adolescent because it was part and parcel with not just one talk, but an ongoing conversation about what was right and wrong, about what was allowed and what was not allowed in our family.

Gary DeGraaf made strong discipline work because he surrounded it with listening and respect. Our point isn't that you should become much tougher with your son. The point is that many fathers and sons are alienated by discipline. It is the job of a father to administer discipline when needed. The times have changed, and most of us don't spank our children much. But we still need to administer discipline, and it is still easy to alienate our children because of that. Good communication helps us discipline our children.

Why? Because when our discipline, whatever form it takes, is part of a lifelong conversation with our kids, they understand the purpose of discipline. They understand our reluctance to discipline, and they know why we have to do it. If we surround discipline with communication, our children will not see it as unjust. They won't resent us (although they probably will resent the discipline). It won't build a wall between us because they will know that discipline is part of the communication.

Good discipline is really just another form of communication. As parents we are trying to make our children hear us, and discipline is much better than shouting at them for an hour at the top of our lungs. When we see disciplining our sons as a way of communicating our values to them, as a way of communicating our beliefs about what is acceptable and what is not, we can see discipline as a way to build our relationship with our sons and not as an obstacle to it.

Expectations

My father's expectations for me have always been high. They weren't unreachable, but often I had to stretch to meet them. That could have been the cause for some resentment toward my dad. I could have thrown up my hands and said, "I just can't live up to what you want from me!" and run off. I didn't do that because Dad communicated those expectations to me in a remarkably positive way, and when the expectations got out of whack, positive communication helped us put things back together.

I remember coming home as a high school junior with a report card that had a "D" seemingly written in neon ink for my parents to notice. I had never gotten a D in my life, and I knew that my parents expected me to get A's and B's, with an emphasis on the former. This D was not going to sit well with them. Sure enough, when they looked at my report card they came right into my bedroom. "Jack, really, a D. Didn't you try at all? I mean, you're smarter than that. We know that you can do better. It's time for you to begin to live up to your potential. . . ."

Oh, by the way, did I mention that report card had six grades on it — the other five being A's. I was angry with my parents for focusing on the D. They were sure that if I could get five A's, I could get six. This could have been a negative situation, because their expectations for me were high and I failed to live up to them. My father was especially disappointed. School was important to him, a college professor, and he wanted his sons to do well. A grade of D, even surrounded by A's, was not acceptable. I could have thrown my hands up in despair at ever pleasing my father, but I didn't. We worked through it with a minimum of fuss. Why? Because my dad knew how to utilize the fathering strength of communication.

He came to me a few hours after his earlier, disappointed visit. "Jack, I'm sorry. I'm really very proud of you, and I know that five A's is wonderful. Most parents would be overjoyed, and I shouldn't have focused on the one negative. But, Jack, you also know that we think you can accomplish anything you want to. You know that your mother and I respect your intelligence and that we expect great things from you because we believe there are great things in you. I guess what I'm saying is that I think you got that D because you hate physiology and didn't study at all for that class. I bet that if you had studied even a little bit you could have gotten a C. Is that true, or am I totally out to lunch about this?"

"No, Dad," I replied, "you're right. I just had trouble actually staying awake in physiology. To be honest, I was bored to tears and didn't put any effort into it."

"Well, I tell you what. I know what it's like to hate a class, but if you hate it so much then you should do well enough in it to at least pass it so you won't have to take it again. If you can pull a C in that class, I'll be satisfied. And, Jack, we really are proud of you."

Expectations are difficult things for sons. Every father has expectations for his son, and sometimes those expectations are out of line with reality. Sometimes those expectations are too high, and instead of challenging the son to do great things, they leave the son feeling defeated before he even starts. Sometimes expectations are a source of great conflict in a relationship. Communication can be the tool that helps us navigate the dangerous shoals of expectation.

By communicating effectively we can reduce the pressure on our sons to achieve our lofty goals for them. The keys to communicating expectations are:

1. Expectations must be clear. My dad is counseling a seventeen-year-old boy. Jason is a senior in high school, and he's frustrated with his parents. They spend most of their time arguing and yelling at each other. One of Jason's main complaints is that his parents won't give him a curfew. He has to ask his parents every day what time they want him to be in, and every day it is different, depending on their mood, or the rotation of the earth, or whatever. Jason has asked repeatedly for a straight curfew so he can plan something with his friends. But his parents refuse, and if he fails to call in they are furious with him. What's the problem here? Expectations are not being clearly communicated. In fact, those expectations are changing nearly every day without warning. That brings us to the second key for communicating expectations.

2. Expectations must be consistent. It isn't fair to constantly

117

change your expectations of your son. It isn't right to leave him wondering what he has to do to be worthy of your trust this time. Be consistent. Jason's dad is doing him and their relationship a grave disservice by not maintaining consistent expectations.

3. Expectations must be reasonable. This doesn't mean that fathers can't expect a lot out of their sons, but our expectations have to be in line with reality. Our kids have to be capable of reaching them. They can be tough, but they can't be impossible.

When these three things are communicated from father to son, expectations don't pose a hazard to the relationship. Instead, they can be an impetus to spur your son on to achievement. Without a clear understanding of your expectations, your son may feel defeated, angry, and resentful.

Failure

Dealing with the failures of our sons is difficult for many of us. We can't believe that our sons won't reach the heights we know they are capable of. We have a tough time coming to grips with the fact that they may make a terrible mistake in their life. We also tend to idealize our sons and see any failures on their part as somebody else's fault; often we see their failures as our fault. We buy into the fallacy that any good thing our sons do is the product of their talent and gifts, but any failure can be traced back to lousy fathering. It is a basic truth that our sons will fail in life. Notice I didn't say fail *at* life, but at some point they will do the wrong thing, sometimes with disastrous results. Without the fathering strength of communication, our relationship with them, nurtured carefully for many years, can easily become a casualty of their failure. With communication, failure can become a springboard to success, a way to grow and to mature.

The difference is in the way we as involved and caring fathers communicate our feelings about their failure to our sons. If we talk and act like it is the end of the world, they will believe that it is the end of the world. If we communicate to them that nothing they can do is bad enough to make us give up on them, then they may have the strength and the will to pick themselves up, dust themselves off, and try again. Too many times I have watched fathers shake their heads in disgust at the normal failures of young children. Too often I have talked to fathers who have given up on their teenage sons after one monumental mistake. Too many times I have heard fathers disparage their grown sons because of their humanness and in this way drive a wedge in their relationship. Be careful what you communicate to your son when he is at his lowest, because he is listening closely to you.

I learned this the hard way with my young son. Jonathon was playing near my computer in my office at home, and he was holding a glass of juice. I warned him that juice wasn't allowed in my office, but he ignored me and then dumped his juice all over my desk, covering three pages of notes and my study Bible with Hi-C. I was angry, and without thinking I lashed out, "Jonathon, I told you not to play in my office with juice. You could have wrecked the computer. I don't think I'm ever going to let you. . . ." I paused in mid-yell because I had caught a glimpse of my son's face. He was mortified. He knew that he had made a mistake and that he had been wrong. He didn't need me to pour hurt on his shame. I looked at him, and his five-year-old eyes welled with tears. "Dad, I'm, I'm, I'm sorry, I didn't. . . ." Then he ran to me and held me close so I wouldn't see his tears. Jonathon knew that he had blown it. He needed reassurance that a few pages of notes and a Bible weren't going to come between us. Your son will need you to communicate the same thing to him when he fails, whether it be in a small, five-year-old way or an enormous, twenty-five-year-old way. We need to communicate our love for our sons during their times of failure.

Values

"Kids today just don't have values any more. That's what's wrong with them." "I'll tell you what's the trouble with young people today — no respect for anybody or anything." "When I was a kid, I knew right from wrong. Today's teenagers don't care."

These statements all came from a group of fathers I was speaking to in the Midwest. I had asked them about their sons' values, or lack thereof, but I hadn't been prepared for the response. These dads vilified their sons. They believed that their sons' values were terrible and getting worse. Only one father out of twenty had something good to say about his son's values. Fathers with good relationships with their sons realize how difficult the rapids of values can be to navigate. We spend a lot more time on this subject in chapter 14, but we need to address it here as well. Without solid communication from you about what is right and wrong, about what is good and just, your son's values and yours will be on a collision course.

Ultimately your son needs to own his values, to sort out what he believes about right and wrong for himself. But I cannot overstate how important it is for us to communicate our values to our sons from the earliest age and at every chance we get. That is one of the things that made Gary DeGraaf's communication with his sons so important. He spent a lot of time telling them what he thought about right and wrong, about heaven and hell, about virtue and vice. And then he listened to them talk through their search for their own values with him as they got older. We have to do the same.

I asked the men at the conference why they felt their sons had such terrible values, why teens in general had these values, and I got a lot of different responses: society, today's permissive culture, liberal Democrats. You name it, they had someone to blame. But then I got kind of hard on them. "How much time did you spend this week at work? Forty hours? Fifty hours? How much time did you spend this week communicating your values to your son?"

We need to take every opportunity to communicate what is important to us to our sons. If we don't teach them, who will?

Paul Hillman is a reflective man with a master's degree in Semitic studies. His son Nathan is pursuing a degree in Scandinavian and German studies. The fact that they spend a lot of time communicating via e-mail doesn't surprise anyone who knows them. Paul is a partner in an editing and design company, while Nathan is a student at the University of Wisconsin. Nathan sums up their special relationship this way: "One of the things I remember about Dad from early on was his deep, deep voice, which could be both scary and entertaining. He loved to create dramas, tell stories, and read books to the kids. He was an incredible storyteller, and I never got bored of listening to him tell stories from his childhood, such as how Uncle Dennis banged his head on a barn door while riding a horse, permanently fixing him as the odd uncle. My favorite may be a story of how a goose clapped onto his belt and Dad ran round and round the house in fright."

Paul and Nathan have spent a great deal of time discussing values and ultimate questions. For years they did it in a fishing boat or in the car on a trip to nowhere special. Now they do it even though an ocean occasionally keeps them apart — by using e-mail. They talk about what matters and what doesn't, and through communication they have safely navigated the shoals of values and begun to dream together.

"I guess we've always enjoyed talking together," Paul says. "When Nathan was a little kid we just enjoyed talking about things." Nathan adds, "Ever since I was quite young we went fishing together, and as some fathers know, while young people sit fidgeting and restless in a wave-rocked boat, fishing is really about life. The analogies between fishing and waiting, fishing and trying new things, fishing and growing up, while one gets cold, wet, sunburned, hungry, bored, excited, or just plain tired, are endless.

"I could always approach Dad and talk to him. He loved the very process of a discussion and was slow to accept black-and-white conclusions, many of which were my own. Over time he and I grew to trust one another due to open communication. The communication continues because of this trust and a mutual fascination in one another's lives."

Paul continues, "We talked a lot and still talk a lot about what it means to be a spiritual person, to follow after God. It's pretty important to me that he works this out in his own life and has a passion for God. Right now, of course, that talk is mostly by e-mail, but it happens almost every night."

Paul Hillman doesn't decry the values of this generation. He has used the tool of communication to pass on his values to Nathan and to encourage him to find his own place in the world, to seek out and own his beliefs and values.

Dreams

I have a dream for my son. I want him to be a football player. I want him to like it as I did, but I want him to play on the first string in high school. Sometimes I even dare dream that one day the head coach of the mighty Michigan Wolverines will knock at my door and ask my son to play for him. As dreams go it's probably not the most realistic, but it is still my dream and it is important to me. I don't tell many people about it because it's kind of silly, but I nurture it inside. And there is nothing wrong with that. But if I don't let go of my dreams for my son and create an atmosphere in which he feels free to communicate his dreams for his life to me, we're headed for trouble.

All of us dream for our sons, and that is good. Sometimes our dreams for them are what get us out of bed in the morning and give us the impetus to go to work for another day. But at some point we have to start listening to our sons tell us their dreams, and if we don't create the space that allows them to dream and to communicate those dreams, we will struggle as fathers. Letting them communicate their dreams to us is not hard. It involves three things: *listening to them, giving them space, communicating our belief in them.* It is as simple as letting them know that we care about what they care about and have nothing better to do than listen to them talk about their hopes and dreams for their life. It means we give them space to create dreams for their lives apart from our dreams for them. It means that we cheer them on every step of the way. Only through this kind of communication can our dreams and our sons' dreams become a source of strength in our relationship together.

Last night I shared with my father some secret dreams I have been harboring in my soul for a long time. They are somewhat farfetched and may seem to silly to most people, but to me they are important. They are also very fragile. The slightest ridicule will kill them, and they need great tending to grow and flourish. When I shared my dreams with Dad he listened, nodded his head, and asked, "How can I help?"

One of the greatest things we can do for our sons is dream with them, and that will happen only when we communicate with them and they feel loved and accepted by us. Nathan Hillman talks about how important that has been in his life. "Dad has long been supportive to me in my life dreams. He never ridiculed me or discouraged me. He would listen and then ask questions more often than give speeches. His concern was that I honestly think about my decisions for myself and not make them under compulsion. This way I came to learn from my mistakes on the one hand and pursue my life dreams with passion and enthusiasm on the other."

Too Important to Skip

Hopefully you understand why we believe communication is such an important strength for fathers to develop. Hopefully you have caught our vision for communication between fathers and sons. Hopefully you understand that it isn't about one special way to talk or to listen; it's about understanding, and that without communication to help you navigate fatherhood the turbulent waters may sink your relationship, or at the very least knock it off course. So we invite you to become master communicators. Use whatever style of communication fits your personality, but build this strength into your fathering so that you too can safely navigate fatherhood.

Father-Son Communication Inventory

Complete the following checklist using the response choices below:

3 = Usually
2 = Sometimes
1 = Seldom

_____ 1. I allow for proper expression of personal opinion.
_____ 2. I do not insist that my son tell me everything.
_____ 3. I seek to understand rather than to be understood.
_____ 4. I admit when I am wrong.

____ 5. I attack the problem, not my son as a person.

____ 6. I use words that build up my son.

____ 7. It's easy for my son to express his ideas and feelings to me.

____ 8. My expectations are clearly communicated to my son.

____ 9. When it is necessary to discipline my son, I clearly explain the reason for the discipline.

____ 10. My son and I dream together.

Scoring: Total your responses.

If you scored 25 or above, you and your son are communicating very well.

If you scored between 20 and 24, you are doing well, but maybe you need to pay a bit more attention to this fathering strength.

Below 20 means you may need some work on your communication skills.

Work especially hard on those items with "Seldom" as a response.

Fathers and Sons Communication Exercises

Exercise #1:

If your son is at least ten years old, ask him to go out to lunch with you. While together ask him to share his dreams with you: "If you could do anything you wanted to do, what would it be?" "When would you like to do this?" "What can we do now to help make this happen in the future?" Then start planning together to help make his dream come true.

Exercise #2:

If your son is under ten years of age, tell him that you have set aside an entire day to be with him. Ask him what he wants to do. Write out a plan for the day together. Follow his agenda and spend the entire day with him. Do a lot of listening throughout the day. Pay special attention to his needs and desires. At the end of the day ask him what was the best part of the day, what he liked the most. Plan to do this again in the near future.

Exercise #3

Have your son take the Father-Son Communication Inventory. Have him rate you and your communication. Ask him how you could improve, based on his answers in the Inventory. Make a commitment to him to work on the "Seldom" responses.

R-E-S-P-E-C-T

...the fathering strength of trust and respect

John Bouma is a successful man. As the president of his own company he has built a nice life for his family. What is even more admirable is that John has built his company without sacrificing his family. And now as his son and executive vice president J.J. will attest, they have become good friends who love and respect each other.

Scott DeGaynor races cars, builds airplanes, and somehow finds time to run his two companies. His son Jonathan found time to earn an MBA from the Wharton School of Business and work with General Motors in new product development, in spite of crashing a few race cars and at least two airplanes with his dad.

I spent part of my childhood at a year-round Christian camp. My father was the camp director, and during the winter he would travel to churches, speaking about the camp, showing slides, and recruiting both campers and camp workers. My brother and I would alternate weekends traveling with him. But it wasn't all fun and games. Dad gave us responsibilities. Our job was to set up and take down the equipment — not a small task. It involved carrying in and setting up the display and all accompanying literature, as well as carrying in and setting up two slide projectors, one large

127

screen, and an overhead projector. We plugged them in and tested them, and if a bulb was burned out we replaced it. If a connection didn't work we fiddled with it. It may not sound like much, but I relished the work. The setup and takedown of the equipment was one of my favorite things to do. Why? Because the equipment was expensive and not easily replaced, and my father trusted me with it. He believed that even at eleven years old I was capable of learning how to work with his equipment. I learned that my father believed in me, that he trusted me, and that he respected me. That belief has been unshaken for nearly twenty years.

Trust and respect are different characteristics, but they are so closely intertwined that for our purposes we will talk about them together. One of the deepest needs we have as men is the need to be respected, to have someone believe in us and our abilities. Along with that is the need to be trusted. We need people in our lives who believe we will do what we say, and we need to prove worthy of that trust. Our self-esteem is built powerfully when we know that our fathers trust us and respect us. By the same token, it is a powerful blow to our self-esteem when our fathers let us know in subtle and sometimes not-so-subtle ways that they can't trust us and they don't respect us. Building your son's self-confidence and belief in himself and his abilities is paramount. If your son goes through high school knowing that you believe in him and that you trust him to do the right thing, his self-esteem will soar — and so do his chances of making right choices.

In almost twelve years of youth ministry, I have noticed almost without exception that kids who are trusted by their parents value that trust and treat it with care. Kids whose parents do not trust them act in untrustworthy ways. Now you may ask, "Which came first, a parent's trust or a child's trustworthy behavior?" I believe, and research bears this out, that parents need to make a conscious choice to trust their children; and when they do that and act like they honestly trust their kids, their children act more trustworthy. Not perfect, mind you, but trustworthy.

The same holds true for respect. When we respect our children, they often do things that build more respect. When we treat our children disrespectfully, they act consistently with that belief. It is as simple as that. But so many fathers look at the world and see all the opportunities their sons have to mess up. And they become fearful, withdrawing the support that their trust and respect bring to their kids and then watch them fall by the wayside, saying all the time, "See, I guess they didn't deserve to be trusted after all." Our hope is that you won't fall into that trap, but that in reading this chapter you will get a glimpse of what true respect and trust are and what they can do for your relationship with your son.

In our research we discovered that mutual trust and respect is an important ingredient in the lives of caring fathers and sons. As fathers we often stress to our children their responsibility to respect and trust us, but often we don't reciprocate that trust and respect. Then we wonder why our relationships are distant or unsatisfying. In this chapter we will look at the lives of two fathers and two sons. These families have built trust and respect into their lives. By looking at them we will identify the four key elements that enable us to build trust and respect, and we will see how building this relationship quality into our lives will make a life-changing difference in our fathering.

John and J.J. Bouma are successful businessmen. Their houses, cars, and busy schedules testify to their success. But after talking with them about their relationship, we got the impression that their business success, while gratifying, wasn't the most important thing to them. What stood out was their mutual respect, trust, and admiration for each other.

John talks about his son and the times they spend together like this: "I feel that our relationship is not just a father-son relationship but a partner relationship. It's also a best friend relationship. We have trust in one another." That trust is apparent as John explains something he did a number of years ago that proved he believed in his sons and in their futures. "J.J. was about twenty-one when he came and asked me for a job, and that was a great day in my life. I remember the tears coming down my cheeks. He grew into his job, and I admire the work he has done for our company. So unknown to him and his brother, I began giving J.J. and Doug my stock in the company. One year after J.J. had been with the company about five years, we were on our annual family ski vacation, and I told J.J. and Doug that they were partners in the business."

"That was a big surprise to me," J.J. says, "and looking back now it means more to me as time goes on than it did at that moment. The thing is, my dad worked hard his entire life to be able to do that. And he didn't do it for material reasons. He did it out of love and respect for my brother and me. It showed me that he trusted me, that he believed in us."

John has gone out of his way to show his boys that he trusts and respects them, and they in turn trust and respect him. When talking to them, it's tough to figure out who trusted whom first. John always has had a deep and abiding respect for J.J. And he has done a terrific job in communicating that respect and trust to him. J.J., on the other hand, isn't shy in praising his father, especially the way his dad runs the business and his family. "I admire Dad's accomplishments in business," J.J. says. "He went through very hard times as a young man, and he's done very well for himself on limited education. But most of all I admire him for the love he's shown his entire family — all of his children — an unconditional love and acceptance. My dad made me feel long ago that I didn't have to be afraid to come to him with a problem. I appreciate and admire his openness and communication; we've been able to share things with each other, to trust each other."

John and J.J. have built a strong relationship around trust and respect. Their relationship is instructive for everyone because it shows two of the key elements in building trust and respect. *First, trust and respect are earned over time.* We want our children to respect us, and often we demand their respect instantly, as if it were an inalienable right, along with life, liberty, and the pursuit of happiness. But respect and trust are earned. They don't happen automatically, and we need to be cognizant that once earned, they also can be destroyed easily. *Trust and respect are built in two simple ways — constancy and honesty.*

Constancy is self-explanatory, but it is difficult to achieve. It means that we as fathers need to be consistent. We need to do what we say we will do, when we say we will do it. Constancy is elusive for many of us because everything else seems to get in the way.

This fall my son, Jonathon, took an interest in football. I'm excited about this because I love football. I love to watch it and like to play it. The downside to his interest in football is that every spare minute Jonathon has he wants to spend playing football outside with me. "Daddy, can we play football outside tomorrow after school?" is his plaintive request every night as I tuck him into bed. And almost every night I answer the same way: "Maybe, Jay. We'll see. Go to sleep now." I almost never end up playing football with him because I'm too busy, or it's too wet, or too cold, or my back hurts, or whatever.

Finally, a few weeks ago, he nailed me down, "Daddy, do you promise to play football with me tomorrow after school?" "Yes, Jonathon, I promise." The next day dawned bright and sunny and warm, a rarity for a Michigan November day. I had completely forgotten my commitment to Jay of the night before when a friend called and asked me if I wanted to squeeze in a round of golf, because the weather was so nice and it would certainly be our last chance to golf. After hanging up the phone I looked around and there was Jonathon, doing his best to choke back tears. "Daddy, are you playing golf today?" "Yeah, I think so, Jay. It's nice outside and probably my last chance." "Oh, OK." Then he turned around, started to cry, and ran into his room. I didn't know what was going on, so I followed him into his bedroom and asked, "Jay, what's wrong? Why the big tears?" "Dad, you promised to play football, but you never do." His words rushed out as tears tumbled down his cheeks for emphasis. The choice was mine: follow through on my commitment I had conveniently forgotten, or chip away at the foundation of my relationship with my five-year-old son. "I'm sorry, Jay. I blew it. I'm staying home, and I'm playing with you. Get your shoes on. Let's go!"

A simple thing, right? Well, not really. Jonathon's ideas about my trustworthiness are built in moments like that one. Thousands of seemingly inconsequential decisions like this build or destroy trust and respect. As fathers, we ignore that fact at great risk. Our consistency, doing what we say we are going to do, following through on our commitments, builds trust.

Consistency also involves being the same person every day. It doesn't mean that we don't have bad days or days when we're disagreeable or irritable. It means that we love our sons every day. We may lose our temper or get angry, but every day, every week, every year our boys need to know that we love them and that by trusting us they aren't taking a huge risk. We will live up to and prove worthy of that trust.

The second part of the equation is honesty. To build trust and respect, we must be honest with our sons. That not only means telling the truth but also living the truth. Ephesians 4:25 tells us to put off falsehood and speak truthfully, but the Greek meaning of that verse involves not just truth-telling but also truth-living. And that is exactly what we must do as fathers.

We must tell the truth about ourselves, our lives, and our world. We must commit to an honest relationship with our sons. No big secrets, nothing hidden in the closet. When they ask us a question, we must give them a straight answer. Our boys deserve our honesty. They have a right to be told the truth. They have a right to have us live truthfully in front of them. If we don't, there is little chance we'll be able to develop trust and respect.

We must exhibit constancy and honesty over a period of time. We can't expect instant trust or instant respect. John and J.J. Bouma have built that respect over a lifetime. J.J.'s obvious respect for his father didn't happen overnight. His father built it over the long days and years of raising J.J. He built it by being faithful to his promises, by doing what he told J.J. he would do. And now, nearing retirement age, John is reaping the rewards for his constancy and honesty: a rich and satisfying relationship with his sons, and their respect and well-earned admiration.

Some of us, frankly, haven't been worthy of trust in the past. Our children know us not as honest, consistent men but as people who lose their temper at every little thing, as men who don't keep their promises, as fathers who always talk a good line but seldom walk what they talk. If that is your situation, don't despair and give up. You can be the man you want to be. You can develop trust and respect in your family, but that won't happen just because you want it to. It will be a process—perhaps painful at times—of your proving over and over again that your word is worth more than "junk bonds," that you will do what you say you will do.

The second principle that J.J. and John's friendship exhibits is that the father must bestow equality and the role of partner on his son. John talks about his son as an equal, as someone whom he has taught and now is teaching him. He talks about what he learns from J.J. and treats him with the respect due a partner. This status bestowal on J.J. is incredibly important. Our children will forever be just that — children — if we do not bestow manhood on them. Other cultures do a much better job than we do of bestowing manhood, with all of its adult privileges and responsibilities, than we do in the West. Our sons need the approval that comes from being treated as a friend and an equal when they grow up.

So many father-son relationships founder when the son enters adulthood because the father cannot let go of his role as protector and parent and move into the role of concerned and loving friend. Our sons are trying to pull loose, to build their own lives, and we still treat them like they are little boys. They need to be treated like men if they are ever to act like men. John was able to do this for J.J. His passing of the stock in his company to his sons was a public rite of passage. J.J. and Doug left for that ski weekend as employees; they returned as owners of the firm.

The father must give permission for equality. The son can do his best to wrest it from him, but it won't work unless the father gives it willingly. When your son is an adult, he needs to be treated as an adult, with respect and love. When you give him permission to be your friend, you create an environment that naturally builds trust and mutual respect. Many fathers and sons in this country have a one-sided view of respect and trust. The father is the object of respect by the son, and the son yearns for the trust of his father, but he never gets it. Respect is a two-way street. After you have earned it as a father, you must bestow it upon your sons. In return, they will reward that action with enormous trust and even more respect.

Our family's mealtimes are chaos. We talk, cajole, argue, lecture, and sometimes disagree. But everything is done with respect for the other people at the table — not necessarily agreement, but respect for them as people. When my friends came over to my house to visit during my college years, they often were amazed at the political, theological, and much-less-weighty matters that were discussed and argued over our table as if the whole world depended on it. When I was nineteen, one friend took me aside after dinner and said, "I can't believe you disagreed with your dad like that. You told him he was wrong, and all he said was 'prove it.' " "Yeah, so what?" I countered. "You don't understand, Jack. Your father treats you like, like maybe you're right. He actually seems to respect your opinion!" I agreed but didn't think that was such a big deal until I met my friend's father. He was an intense man who overpowered his son at every turn. He showed absolutely no regard for his son's viewpoint or the thoughts behind the viewpoint. After all, he was the father, and the father was in charge. That attitude will prevent us from enjoying the rich and full relationship we crave with our sons. We must treat them respect, bestowing the rights and privileges of manhood on them. We must treat them as equals, listening to them, understanding them, and trusting them.

Scott and Jonathan DeGaynor grew up building and racing cars together, building and flying airplanes together, and restoring old cars. During those hundreds of hours together, they also built a relationship that has stood the test of time and is growing stronger as they grow older. According to them, their secret is simple— mutual admiration.

Jonathan talks about the trust and respect his father showed him from the time he was very young. "Dad entrusted me with a lot of responsibility. Whether it was being in business meetings for his leasing company when I was ten years old, his putting me out on the road for the company cleaning machines and collecting money at sixteen or seventeen years old, putting me behind the wheel of one of his trucks at eighteen, entrusting me with handling the bagging of ice at a certain period of time [they were in the ice business], or trusting me with any of his valuable cars, he believed in me. And some of the best opportunities to learn came when I made a mistake."

Jonathan continues, "He never gave up on me even when I

really messed up. Probably the best example of that was when, with a friend of ours, we restored a 1958 Corvette. One of my father's favorite sayings is, 'If we borrow something from somebody else, and break it, we'll fix it.' I was home from college for the summer, and I had taken one of our cars out, a nice old car, but evidently not nice enough for me. So I stopped at our friend's house and without asking anybody took the Corvette. Now that probably wouldn't have been any problem, but I proceeded to blow the engine that night. So I had to come home, with my dad working out in the barn, and tell him what I had done. Well, there was no way to get around it, no way for me to solve this problem on my own. That was probably one of the toughest things I ever had to do, and the way he handled it was amazing. He was dead calm. He said, 'Let's go get the car and fix it.' The fact that I had to face up to it tore me apart, and the fact that I had let him down, after he had entrusted me with so much.

"That just exemplifies the way our relationship grew. There was always trust both ways. I once got two speeding tickets in four days, and I remember how he handled that. We both went down to the secretary of state's office and sat down with them. He told them, 'You don't need to put him on restricted license. I will do that. I will take care of it and make sure this problem is solved,' and he did. So we've always had respect for each other, strong respect, justified by the way he ran his life, his family, his marriage, and his business."

Talk about respect and trust! Jonathan learned early that his father would follow through. He learned early that his father would do what he said he would do. He learned early that words such as *respect* and *trust* meant something and that his father had confidence in him, believed in him, and wouldn't give up on him. He also learned an important lesson in that when he messed up, his father made him face the consequences but didn't withdraw his respect and trust.

And that is our third key to building a trusting respectful relationship: Be liberal with forgiveness. Jonathan learned that his father would not give up on him because of one incident or even because of ten incidents; and having his father believe in him, trust him after every miscue, and give him more responsibility probably did more to build Jonathan into a man of integrity and honesty than any lecture or browbeating would have accomplished. That is a hard concept to put into practice, but it is crucial. If we stop believing in our sons because they are human and fail, they will stop believing in themselves. And then we will be in for trouble. Be generous with your forgiveness. Don't pull your trust from your son because he has betrayed it. Explain how much it hurts to have that trust betrayed. Explain how important it is to you as a father to place your trust in your son, and explain to him what a weighty responsibility that trust is. But don't give up on your son too soon.

I was speaking with a father the other day who said that his dad had told him he could help him on the farm by driving the tractor when he turned thirteen. But in his first afternoon in the field, the boy rode the clutch too hard and burned it out. His father never let him sit on the tractor again. That boy, now with three sons of his own, told me, "I'm never going to quit believing in my boys, because I know what that feels like, and I understand the hurt that comes when your father thinks very little of you, his own son."

Scott DeGaynor talked with us about the legacy he'd like to leave behind for Jonathan. "I'd like Jonathan — and I think he's already caught a lot of it — to be honest, to be a man of integrity who cares about his family. Whatever he does through his whole career, if he can walk out the door with his head held high, and do the same thing with his family, that's what I'd like to see him live out. That's the legacy for me."

"I learned a lot from Dad about that," Jonathan concurs. "He's as honest as the day is long. He is as caring as any father I've ever come in contact with. The emotion that he is able to show, and the stability that he portrays through our family life and in tremendous challenges in business, those are things I take with me from our relationship."

Jonathan's respect for his father and his accomplishments, both in his family and his business, are obvious. Equally obvious when speaking with Scott is the pride he takes in Jonathan's achievements, and the trust and respect he feels for Jonathan. He showed this to Jonathan when he was young by giving him responsibilities and expecting Jonathan to live up to them. *That is the fourth key to building trust and respect in a father-son relationship: Give responsibility equal to the trust and respect.*

Many fathers tell their sons they are trusted and respected; not as many fathers actually act as if they trust and respect their sons. It is one thing to talk about trusting and respecting and quite another to live out that trust and respect. Scott proved his trust and respect for his son by giving him valuable opportunities. He gave him responsibility that equaled his stated respect and trust, and although Jonathan, by his own admission, wasn't a perfect kid, he lived up to his father's trust and proved worthy of the respect. If we don't give our kids any opportunities to fail, they also will be bereft of opportunities to succeed. True responsibility carries no guarantees. Our sons might mess up. They may prove they still have a long way to go. But without the opportunity to succeed, to try to prove worthy of our trust, they will never build the confidence and self-esteem that warrant our trust in them and our respect for them.

At the beginning of this chapter I marveled that my father gave me the responsibility of taking care of the equipment for his presentations. In that time I never dropped an overhead projector or blew up the slide projector. But evidently I wasn't the only person who marveled at the trust and respect my father was showing me. Our assistant director was an older man, and I remember him speaking with Dad one Sunday afternoon while I was unloading the equipment from our trip. He told my father he didn't think it was right for an eleven-year-old boy to carry that equipment and set it up. He told Dad that if I dropped or broke anything, he, the assistant director, would tell the board of directors that it was my dad's responsibility to pay for it. He had been warned. I'll never forget what my father said to that man. He smiled, looked at me hauling in the display case, and said, "That's OK. My boys know what they are doing. I believe I'll take that chance." Wow! What a vote of confidence from my father. After hearing that, I walked a little straighter and held my head up higher, because my father believed in me.

Building trust and respect into our relationship with our sons isn't an easy task. It is vitally important, however, if we want to build a friendship that will last a lifetime. Remember the keys to building trust and respect:

1. *Trust and respect are earned over a period of time.*

2. *The father must bestow equality and the role of partner and friend on his son.*

3. *Be liberal with forgiveness and second chances.*

4. *Give responsibility equal to the trust and respect.*

Trust and Respect Self-Check

Use the following self-check to see how you are doing at building the fathering strength of trust and respect.

	Often	**Sometimes**	**Seldom**
1. I give my son challenging, age-appropriate tasks that demand trust on my part.	____	____	____
2. I teach my son how to properly care for and maintain equipment.	____	____	____
3. I don't give up on my son easily, but I give him a second chance to do something right.	____	____	____
4. I give my son age-appropriate tasks to perform along with sufficient instruction to complete the task.	____	____	____

138

5. I believe in my son.   ____   ____   ____

6. I give my son the
   opportunity to be
   successful.   ____   ____   ____

7. I allow my son to fail at
   certain tasks without
   retribution.   ____   ____   ____

8. I am honest with my son. ____   ____   ____

9. My conduct is consistent
   with my creed.   ____   ____   ____

Relationship-Building Activity

Doing things with your son, allowing him to work with you, to
help you, to accomplish a task is one of the best ways to build
trust and respect into your relationship. Use the following guide-
lines to help you design a relationship-building activity.

1. List several age-appropriate projects you and your son can do
   together.

_____

_____

_____

_____

_____

2. Talk with your son to get his input on the projects. Try to incorporate his ideas.
3. Allow him to work with you on the projects. Give him important tasks to complete. Help him when necessary, but do not complete his tasks for him.
4. Set aside time on your calendar now to work on these projects and tell your son about the time you have set aside. This will make you accountable.
5. Follow through!

Chapter Ten

The Main Event

...the fathering strength of conflict resolution

Les and Chad Vanden Heuvel share a love for the outdoors and hunting. Les works in telecommunications; his son Chad has followed his instincts and works outdoors as a nurseryman. Together they have learned how to handle the conflict between them and build a lasting friendship.

Les and Chad Vanden Heuvel look back on Chad's teenage years and chuckle with each other. It was not an easy time in their family. They are both strong-willed people, and during that time their wills were often in direct opposition to each other. Chad puts it this way: "[We fought about] anything and everything. It was more about principles. I think it must be a genetic thing, but we were really bullheaded in our views." Les adds, "When a kid graduates from high school, he thinks he's got all the answers, just like I thought I had all the answers. But because I've been a little longer on the face of the earth, I see the problems ahead, and one of the biggest things we butted heads on was his time coming home.

"He would come in really late, and to be honest, it bothered his mother more than it bothered me, because I could sleep through it. But she would wake me up and say, 'Look at this. It's 1:00 A.M. and Chad's not home.' We knew where he was—he was with his girlfriend. So there were problems with them spending so much time together, and we butted heads about that too. Now that he's married we found out that most of the time she had fallen asleep and he was on the floor with the dog, and that was it.

"It was kind of a controlling thing. I wanted control [over my son], but I knew I couldn't have it, and that was the frustrating part about it. So you butt heads, and that raises your hackles in a hurry."

"I was staying out late. My curfew was 12:30 A.M.," Chad says, "and I would think, *I'm going to be out till 12:31 just to prove that I'm responsible. I can show you that I'm able to do that.*"

"So many times Chad would say, 'Look at me. Am I so bad compared to other kids?' And that would kind of get to me too. We weren't comparing him with other kids. We were trying to do what we thought was right, but kids don't always see it that way. And I didn't either when I was growing up. My folks said a lot of that stuff to me that I didn't think made sense, but it makes a lot of sense now."

It would have been easy for two strong, intelligent people like the Vanden Heuvels to stay angry at each other, to let the conflict in their relationship rip them apart. But they didn't let that happen. Chad and Les are the friends they are today because early on in their life together they developed the fathering strength of conflict resolution. And that has enabled them to make it through the storms of adolescence, to sail through those rough seas to the relative tranquility of adulthood with their relationship intact.

"Early on Chad and I did have a few problems," Les says. "We were a lot alike, and neither one wanted to give in sometimes. But we learned. It really was the Lord who spoke to me. He said, 'Hey, you're not getting anywhere, you know. He's getting on in his teen years.' Chad's quite a debater, and he likes to get the last word and so do I. Finally I realized, hey, we're a lot alike. We're not going to gain anything like this. I'm going to listen to him more. Maybe I've got to see him in a different light. Maybe what he's saying isn't all wrong. Maybe Dad's going to have to change his attitude a little bit. It really helped. We had some good arguments when he was growing up, and I wondered how everything would turn out. But the next day we were as close as we were the day before. It started to get a lot better when we sat down and said, 'Let's start listening to each other more.'

"I learned that for us listening is a key. You can go miles by listening; say less and listen more. I've found out there's so much I don't know. At first it was like, 'OK, I'll give you your chance to speak.' I was allowing him his chance to speak, but I wasn't listening. That's not our way anymore."

"We've come along way," adds Chad. "And I really respect my dad. It's been a neat transition now that I'm married. You go from only a father-son relationship to now father-son-friends. I think that's neat because now I call him up and say, 'Let's go out for coffee,' or, 'What are you doing tonight?' It's fun just to get together and do nothing."

Conflict is a normal part of every father-son relationship. Some fathers and sons learn how to handle conflict, fights, anger, and tough times effectively and positively. Some fathers and sons don't. If you want to grow close to your son, if you want your relationship not only to survive into your son's adulthood but to thrive all the way there, then you must build the fathering strength of conflict resolution into your life.

Ten Things You Need to Know about Fighting with Your Son

The following ten observations come from my father's twenty years of family counseling and thirty years of fathering sons.

1. Fighting is normal and inevitable. If you breathe and have opinions and your son breathes and has opinions, you will fight. We use the word *fight* on purpose. Conflict is a nice, sanitized way of viewing it, but what we are talking about is what happens between fathers and sons every day — fights. Hopefully, your fights are not physical brawls, and they may consist of long periods of punishing silence or aloofness, but they are still fights. Everybody fights. We fight because we want our way. We fight because we don't get our way. We fight because we are hurt and because we don't want to be hurt. If two people live together, they will find a

143

lot of reasons to fight. Some fathers and sons are especially good at finding new things to fight about; most of us just have the same two or three fights over and over. It's OK. It's normal to fight.

As your son grows into adolescence and starts to build his own identity, conflict will come. And no matter how strong your relationship is, there will be periods of struggle. Realize that conflict is normal and inevitable in any relationship. The best fathers and sons still have times of difficulty.

2. Fighting isn't failure. Many of us have bought into a vision of families that just doesn't square with reality. In that vision fathers come home from work and are greeted by their dutiful sons at the front door. Each son is of course groomed impeccably, with short hair, and is dressed like he is on his way to church. In our vision sons ask respectfully and fathers are never tired or frustrated or afraid. They never lose their cool and are never angry with their sons, and their sons are never surly or unresponsive.

When our lives don't fit that ideal, when we are angry and fight with our sons and they fight with us, when frustration is the dominant theme of our relationship, we feel like we have failed. It isn't true. Fighting isn't failure. It is the natural process of working out differences. Conflict doesn't have to be the end of the world and doesn't have to tear your family apart. The key is to learn how to fight without tearing the other person down or destroying your relationship. When you and your son exchange angry words or spend a day or two in silence, you haven't failed as a father and your relationship isn't ruined forever.

Forget the fairy tale. I don't live it with my father or my son. I prefer the real world of snarls and hasty words, of forgiveness and the joy of working out differences honestly and respectfully.

3. Conflict can lead to growth. Conflict and the process of resolving it can be an impetus for personal growth. It can cause us to look at our lives and to assess what kind of people we want to be and to take the steps necessary to be that kind of person. Shortly after I had begun my ministry many years ago, a father was talking to me about his son and a recent fight they had. "He accused me of saying no all the time because it was easier. My son yelled it at me and I was furious with him. I grounded him and sent him to his room, but when I thought about it I realized there was more than just a grain of truth in what he was saying. I began to think, *Is that the kind of dad I want to be?* The answer of course was no. That fight really opened my eyes."

4. Unresolved conflict stymies personal growth. Just as resolving conflict and working through it can help us grow, conflict that simmers unresolved will hinder our personal growth. If we don't deal with conflict it can become a prison for us, holding us and our sons hostage to anger, resentment, and bitterness. It is the sad truth that in a combined thirty-plus years of ministry to families, Dad and I have seen too many fathers and sons who have given up trying to resolve the conflict in their lives. They are resigned to its presence, unresolved and seething in their relationship. Needless to say these men are not growing personally; the obstacle of unresolved conflict stands in their way.

My father had a man in his office last week who had just buried his father. In my dad's office he cried for the first time as an adult, the tears bursting in a flood down his careworn face. "I didn't speak to my dad for almost twenty years," he said. "I don't even remember why we were angry at each other. After a while it didn't matter anymore. My anger almost destroyed my marriage and severely damaged my relationship with my own son. Now my father is gone, and I can never bring those years back. I have wasted so much time."

5. Unresolved conflict creates emotional distance between you and your son. Many of us have fights and then go to bed, never deal with the issue, and then get up in the morning and go about our business as if it never happened. This is not a good idea if you want to build a close friendship with your son. Eventually the unresolved conflict, the fights that never really ended, create distance between the two of you. And before you know it you are so far apart you have to shout to be heard, and that often is the only kind of communication you engage in.

One of the central points of this chapter is that fighting isn't failure and conflict is normal, but it must be dealt with effectively and positively. If it isn't, it will become a drag on your relationship, holding you back from true intimacy and friendship.

6. Resolving conflict contributes to building a cohesive relationship with your son. Every time you fight and deal with that fight in a positive and effective way, bringing it to resolution, you have scored another point for emotional closeness. There is something powerfully rewarding and edifying about working through difficulties with your son. When you come through the other side, you find that you are closer than before, that the conflict has actually strengthened your relationship. Knowing that you can handle difficulties brings a great deal of confidence to your relationship. You and you son know that whatever is said won't destroy your relationship because you can handle fights without hurting each other. You have proven that difficulties aren't the end of your friendship, and in that confidence you will actually fight less, finding it rewarding when you do fight and manage to work it out.

7. Conflict often involves personal values. Many fathers and sons fight about values. They fight about what is and what is not important in life. They fight about what constitutes a good life, what is "right and wrong," and morality. They fight about spiritual and theological issues. These fights about personal values are often the most bitter and damaging, because values define who we are and how we live. When our sons challenge our values, we react strongly and usually negatively. Values are a big deal to us and they should be. But it is important to realize that our sons need to own their own values. They can't get by on what they have inherited from us, no matter how much we want to believe otherwise. So we need to follow Les Vanden Heuval's advice and listen to our sons and look at things from their perspective.

Give yourself the freedom to disagree with each other without hurting each other. In the crucial area of values, that is a key relationship survival tip.

8. Conflict is often rooted in fear. We wrote an entire book about this subject (*Family Fears*, Victor Books, 1994), but it needs to be said again briefly in this context. One of the root causes of conflict is fear. It often lies behind the anger and frustration that seem to plague our relationships with our sons: fear that he won't turn out right; fear that he will make a life-dominating mistake; fear that he will reject our values and beliefs; fear that we have failed as fathers. These are real issues in many families, and often a trip to a friend, pastor, or counselor to talk about your fears will help you sort this out. If you suspect that fear is behind much of your conflict, we recommend picking up a copy of *Family Fears*. In it you will find practical suggestions to help you work through your fear and build a new, confident love with your son.

9. Many of us don't know how to resolve conflict. This is a serious problem for many men. We never learned appropriate ways to work out disagreements. Many men never had it modeled to them, and when I talk about resolving conflict positively and effectively, you grimace and put the book down because I'm speaking a foreign language to you. That's OK. Don't give up. The last few pages of this chapter will help you get a handle on your style of handling conflict, and then we'll teach you how to begin to resolve conflict with your son.

It is important to admit this if it is true of you and your family. By admitting that you don't know how to handle conflict, you give yourself the opportunity to learn and the freedom to try and fail and try and fail again. If you haven't seen effective conflict resolution, then you can't be expected to automatically know how to deal with a fight. You need to learn how to reach resolution.

10. Continual fighting over a variety of issues is often a symptom of a deeper problem. No, we aren't reaching into the realm of psychobabble here. We aren't talking about repressed memories or hypnosis-induced inner child searching. What we mean is that if your life is characterized by continual conflict, there are probably some other issues that need to be dealt with. It doesn't mean you are sick or hopeless, but that some areas of your life need attention. We recommend seeking out a pastor or Christian counselor to help you deal with those issues.

The Challenge

The challenge for us as fathers who want to build lifelong friendships with our sons, friendships that stand the test of time and weather the storms of adolescence, is to build a way of dealing with conflict into our relationship with our sons. The Bible has some terrific words for fathers on this subject. In Romans 12 Paul urges us to "live in harmony with one another. . . . Do not repay anyone evil for evil. Be careful to do what is right in the eyes of everybody. If it is possible, as far as it depends on you, live at peace with everyone" (vv. 16-18).

In trying to accomplish that difficult task with our sons, the first thing we must do is figure out how we deal with conflict. All of us have our own style of handling conflict. Recognizing our natural style is extremely important to resolving fights with our sons.

The following diagram is from James Fairfield's great book on conflict, *When You Don't Agree* (Herald Press, 1977, p. 231). It is reprinted here with their permission and will help us figure out how we handle conflict. We'll refer to the diagram throughout the next couple of pages, so take a moment to look at it now.

Styles of
Handling Conflict

High concern for relationship

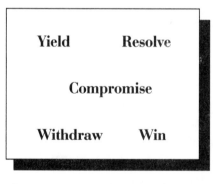

Low in

achieved

needs

Yield   Resolve

Compromise

Withdraw   Win

High in

achieved

needs

Low concern for relationship

How Do You Fight?

Some of us handle conflict by *yielding.* When we yield we just give up and let the other person have his way. Often teenagers deal with conflict in this manner. They can't make themselves heard, and they are tired of the consequences of rocking the boat, so they give in. But it is not just students who yield. Many parents quit on their relationship as well.

Many of us deal with fights and disagreements by *withdrawing*. We can do that either emotionally, withdrawing from the relationship, refusing to fight or engage, or we can do that physically during a fight, walking into another room, or leaving the house. Some of us withdraw physically by leaving home for good, abandoning our families to avoid dealing with conflict. Most often we withdraw by refusing to discuss the issue, by emotionally pulling ourselves out of the fight before it is resolved.

Winning seems to be a common male way of handling conflict. In this style of fighting we keep fighting until we wear out the other person and get our way. Sometimes we are more skillful verbally, and sometimes we are more cruel. It doesn't matter to us winners. What matters is that we prove we are right. My father's predominant conflict management style is winning. So is mine. That is why we fought a lot.

When we *resolve* we try to bring conflict to a mutually beneficial end. Few of us are natural resolvers. Most of us resolve only as a last resort. It is more learned behavior than natural instinct. Realize that resolution to everybody's satisfaction is not always possible.

Compromisers often confuse themselves with resolvers. They think that by trying a little of yours and a little of mine they can work out a solution, but compromise isn't always right or even good for a relationship. Sometimes a little of each is worse than one or the other. Sometimes we compromise because we don't want to thrash out the true issue, so we immediately seek an easy solution. Unfortunately, that isn't always the best way to deal with conflict. Nevertheless, the attitude of compromise, a willingness to give in a little and to try to reach resolution, is incredibly valuable.

If you look closely at the diagram you'll see that yielding and withdrawing are low in achieved needs. That means if we continually deal with conflict in that way we won't get what we need out of a relationship. If our sons are continually forced to yield to us, their needs will be unmet. And that won't go on forever. Sooner or later our sons will stand up for what they need, although they may do so by slipping quietly out the back door, never to return.

Resolving and winning are high in achieved needs. Winners get what they want. They feel good because their needs have been met. If you look at the bottom part of the diagram, you'll realize that in the process of winning they have shown little concern for the relationship with their sons. Their needs took precedence, and the relationship wasn't as valuable to them.

Those of us who withdraw from conflict are showing a similar lack of concern for the relationship. When we refuse to engage our sons, or they refuse to engage us, we are saying that the relationship isn't important enough to risk an argument over.

Yielders show a high concern for the relationship. Often they yield because they are afraid if they don't it will irreparably damage the father-son relationship. In the process they forfeit their own emotional well-being and give up on their own needs.

Resolvers have the best of both worlds. In resolution the relationship is valued and needs are achieved. Certainly, that is what we all need to strive for.

As you look at this diagram you may think, *Hey, I'm none of those,* or even more likely, *Hey, I do all of that stuff.* That is true, but most of us have a dominant style, so taking a few moments to show this diagram to your family and asking them where you are on it can be an eye-opener.

I was explaining this model at a retreat a few years ago, and after my talk a pastor came up to me. He said that he had gone through this exercise with his family and was a little disturbed by what he had learned. He had confidently placed himself among the resolvers, but when he went around and asked his family, his wife calmly told him he liked to win. He looked at his son, who said, "Dad, it's true. You always have to win." He turned with a longing look to his daughter, hoping she would back him up. She just shook her head, "Sorry, Dad, but you can't bear not to win." The pastor looked at his family and said, "But you don't mind, do you?"

This exercise is important because it shows us where we are. It helps us see whether we truly act like we value our relationship with our son and whether we value his needs. Because it can be such an eye-opener, we advise you to take a few minutes and share this with your son if he is junior high age or older. If he isn't, share this with your wife or a close friend who knows you well and will be honest with you. The point is not to condemn you but to help you become aware of your conflict management style.

After you figure out where you are, ask yourself the tough questions and form a plan of action to help you become more oriented toward resolution. You don't have to get there overnight. After all, I teach this stuff, and I still like to win. My dad has taught this stuff for fifteen years, and he still likes to win. We are all on a journey and we haven't arrived.

How to Enjoy Fighting with Your Son

We can't guarantee that you'll enjoy your fights, but by following this model for resolving conflict your fights will be more productive and less hurtful, and resolution will become a part of your fathering style.

1. Find an appropriate time and place to deal with it. A cardinal rule for fathers and fights: when your son staggers into the house drunk at 3:00 A.M., and you've been up alternately furious and beside yourself with anxiety, that is not an appropriate time or place to discuss the matter. Wait until you are rested and rational, and the same is true for your son. Ask him to set a time and a place where he is comfortable to deal with the issues.

2. Clearly define the issue. Have you ever been in the middle of a fight and forgotten what the real problem was? I have and it's kind of embarrassing. Of course, usually that's not enough to keep us from continuing the fight. Figure out what the real issue is. Are you angry at your son because he was late? Because being late shows a lack of respect for you and your rules? Or because you are worried about what he was doing with his girlfriend while he was out? Those are all different issues, and until you clearly define the problem you won't solve it. Many times you and your son are fighting about entirely different things. That is a waste of time. Stop and define the issue first.

3. List some possible solutions. When listing some possible solutions to the conflict you must list at least three — your solution, his solution, and something else. If it is just "my way or the highway," the fight may never end. I remember a father and son in my office a few years ago arguing about church attendance. The son wanted to go to his girlfriend's church; the father wanted his son to go to church with the family. They argued for almost an hour, getting nowhere fast. I suggested that the son go to church in the morning with his parents and at night with his girlfriend. They agreed and the fight was over.

The more solutions you can come up with, the better your chance to resolve the conflict. So spend some time on this step. Brainstorm. You might even find yourself having fun. (Be careful, though. We wouldn't want that to happen. This is a fight, remember?)

4. Choose the best solution. Together (and that is a key), choose the best possible solution. The best solution is usually a double win, where both parties or all three parties get some of their needs met. If you insist on winning this is a tough step for you, because the double win, where I get at least part of what I need and you get at least part of what you need, may not satisfy your need to win. Get past that and choose the solution that is beneficial to both you and your son, and do it in conjunction with him. Don't impose it on him. Make him an integral part of the process, even at a young age.

5. Just do it. Implement the solution. I don't know how many times I've been in a fight with my father and we have just about worked the whole thing out when I stop short of implementing the solution. I may have thought of it, but I dive back into the argument, hoping to get my way entirely. Resist that temptation. Put your solution to work in your relationship, and then enjoy the benefits of resolved conflict in your life.

No Magic Wand

You'll notice that our way of handling fights involves some tough work. There are no magic ways to deal with conflict, no waving of wands to make our disagreements go away. It takes a lot of commitment to work out disagreements, to fight through to a solution, to resolve conflict. But don't let that deter you. Your son is worth it. Your friendship with him is worth it. Do what it takes and you will strengthen your relationship every time you fight, growing closer together, building a lifetime friendship.

How Do You Fight? Checklist

After each of the following techniques, indicate whether you use it frequently, occasionally, or rarely. Afterward have your son do this exercise (help him if he is younger), then talk about it together.

	Frequently	Occasionally	Rarely
1. Avoid the person.	____	____	____
2. Change the subject.	____	____	____
3. Try to understand the other person's point of view.	____	____	____
4. Try to turn the fight into a joke.	____	____	____
5. Admit you are wrong even if you do not believe you are.	____	____	____
6. Give in.	____	____	____
7. Apologize.	____	____	____
8. Try to find out specifically what you agree and disagree on to narrow the conflict.	____	____	____

153

9. Try to compromise. _____ _____ _____

10. Pretend to agree. _____ _____ _____

11. Get another person to mediate, deciding who is right. _____ _____ _____

12. Threaten the other person. _____ _____ _____

13. Fight it out physically. _____ _____ _____

14. Whine or complain until you get your way. _____ _____ _____

15. Play the martyr. Give in but let the other person know how much you are suffering. _____ _____ _____

Chapter Eleven

Seventy Times Seven

...the fathering strength of forgiveness

He drove past his house with his headlights off and the engine running slowly but quietly. He looked carefully into the 2:00 A.M. darkness. Sure enough, there they were. The police were waiting for him in the driveway of his father's house. He looked briefly at the big, white farmhouse. Inside there was a light on. Probably his mom and dad sitting at the kitchen table, a cup of coffee or tea in their hands, knowing the police were looking yet again for their oldest son.

Their son drove off into the darkness. Up the hill, past the family farm, he turned on the headlights, raced the engine, and accelerated to almost 100 miles per hour on that deserted country road. It didn't feel too good knowing that his parents had to deal with the police in their driveway, but speed and its adrenaline took an edge off of his guilt. So he drove into the night, like so many other nights before, looking for a fight, for his buddies, for a drink.

His parents looked at the clock and realized that their oldest son probably wasn't coming home. They stepped out onto the porch and waved at the deputy trying to stay awake in his car. They knew him well. Theirs was a small town, and everyone knew about their son.

The papers from across the state had heralded his latest arrest, "Leader of swamp gang nabbed!" It was funny because there was no "swamp gang"—just a few guys who liked to drive fast, steal things for the thrill of it, and give the police a hard time. The last time he'd been arrested something had seemed to change in their son. He was less fun-loving, more grim, and angry all the time. He was talking about being set up and how he was going to get "those guys." His dad knew he was talking about the sheriff. He knew that his son felt the sheriff had framed him. The father could hardly blame the sheriff. His son had gotten away with so much taunting and mocking of local law enforcement officials that it was only a matter of time before they put him away for good, even if they had to trump up the charge and pay off the defense attorney. But it wasn't sitting so well with his son. He had gotten off at the last minute on a technicality, but he had been only a few words away from a fifteen-year stint in a maximum security prison for a crime he didn't commit. And he was angry.

The father would have had an even more difficult time sleeping that night had he been able to read his son's thoughts. They were thoughts of revenge, of taking a man's life. This young, tough guy felt betrayed by the system. Sure, he had gotten away with a lot of things, but that didn't make it right for the sheriff to make it a personal thing and go after him beyond the bounds of the law. *Well,* the young criminal thought, *if he wants it personal, I can make it personal.* This young hoodlum had been raised on a farm and had hunted since he was able to carry a gun. An exceptional shot, he had a specially made 25-06 rifle, a flat-shooting rifle with which he had killed antelope on a hunting trip out west from more than 500 yards away. His mind began to race. He could sit on the top of a certain building, and when the sheriff walked out his front door, "click"—a simple pull of the trigger and the personal vendetta against him would be history. As the criminal began to plan his crime, a thought slowly came over him. *I can't kill this man with my rifle. It is the only gun like it for a hundred miles. They will know who shot him and why.*

So again as he drove along the back roads he began to think. Experienced at blasting stumps out of fields, he knew how to use dynamite and knew how to get his hands on it. It wouldn't be a big problem to wire the sheriff's car so that when he turned the ignition he would complete a circuit and blow himself up. That was a satisfying thought, but he wondered, *What if someone else gets in the car? I don't want to kill an innocent person.* And so he thought on until he finally fell asleep.

The criminal's father was beside himself. A gentle, loving man, he didn't know what to do about his oldest son. The last few years had been tough on him and his wife as they watched their son quit school and take up with a rough crowd. They had convinced themselves that their son was being influenced by his friends to do wrong, to break the law, to get into trouble. A more troubling realization was starting to dawn on them — that their son was actually the ringleader and the chief troublemaker. Oh, how they grieved for him. How many times had they sat up late, just staring quietly into their coffee cups, wondering what would become of their boy. He had been so full of life and laughter, a smart, even gifted student, but he seemed to be on an unending search for thrills. Eventually, school just bored him too much, so he quit. They knew he had been spending a lot of time driving recklessly or drinking and fighting.

The first time the deputy sheriff had appeared on their doorstep with the news that their son was in jail had been tough. Now, so many little trips to the county jail later, they weren't even surprised — just saddened and increasingly angered by their son's behavior. Things had really deteriorated since he had been picked up for breaking and entering. It was the second time in less than a year that he was to stand trial for breaking and entering, and he was still on probation. It looked as if he were headed to the state penitentiary for a long time. But then the technicality came up and their son was free. But he was angrier, determined to get those who had set him up.

The father began to think of all the times they had been fishing together, of all the hours spent waiting for a fish to rise to the bait, of the talks and the laughter, the joy they had shared together. *Can I forgive my son for the pain he has brought into my life?* he wondered as he set out for another day in the celery fields.

His son slowly lost his desire to kill the sheriff. He never followed up on any of his plans. He didn't exactly improve his lifestyle and still was in trouble with the law regularly, but he had met a girl. She was funny, loud, and sexy. They were in love and were going to get married. So the criminal shaped up a little bit. He got a real job and tried to get ready for the birth of a baby. Their first house as a married couple was across the field from a deacon in the Baptist church. This deacon decided the criminal needed Jesus, so he got to know his new, less-than-desirable neighbor. They became good friends. They rode motorcycles together, hunted together, and fished together. The deacon even went so far as to buy a motorcycle in a wash tub, every nut and bolt apart, knowing that his new criminal friend loved to work on bikes and couldn't resist a challenge. They spent hours together building that bike, and over those hours the deacon shared Jesus with the criminal. And one day the criminal got down on his knees and awkwardly asked Jesus to come into his life. Three days later I was born. That criminal was my father, his long-suffering dad, my grandpa.

I talked to my grandpa many times about my dad. I asked him what it felt like to have a son who was so obviously going the wrong direction. He would speak of how much it hurt, but only for a moment or two. Then he would quickly change the subject and speak of how proud he was of my dad, of how my father had turned out so wonderfully. One day when I was in my teens, angry at my own father, I asked my grandpa how he could forgive my dad for the things he had done, for the shame and embarrassment he had brought to the family. My grandpa's reply was simple, "He was always my son. I forgave him without thinking about it. I never held anything against him. He was my son, and I loved him."

Forgiveness is a powerful force in the relationship between a father and a son. There will be many times when the son hurts his father, sometimes through what he says, sometimes by what he does, often with a cutting tone or lack of respect. It is a wise father who cultivates an attitude and lifestyle of forgiveness. There are times when our fathers have hurt us or wronged us. There will be times when we hurt our sons and don't give them justice or fairness. Forgiveness on the part of our sons will help our relationship stay strong.

Our Forgiving Father

Forgiveness is not easy. When we are hurt by others it is far from natural for us to forgive them, to remain open with them, possibly only to be hurt again. Our natural reaction is to withdraw from the relationship emotionally, to want revenge, to hurt them as they have hurt us.

The good news is that although forgiving is tough to do, we are not without a model. There is One who has gone before us to chart a course for forgiveness, and by following His lead our lives can become characterized by a forgiving spirit. Our Father God, who loves us and calls us by name, has been hurt by us many times. You and I have sinned. We have literally fallen short of or missed the mark, and our sin grieves our Heavenly Father. But His response to our sin, to the pain we bring Him, is not retaliation, not withdrawal, but the open hand of complete forgiveness. And this is the model we must follow, but we must first live it.

It is difficult to be a forgiving father when we are not forgiven ourselves. It is well and good to talk about it, but until we have felt the shower of redemption that is forgiveness, we will have a difficult time extending it to our sons. All of us need to first understand and live in the forgiveness of the fathering God. The truth of God's forgiving me has had the deepest and most profound impact on my life. The fact that the fathering God, who made me and knows me, is waiting with open hands to receive me back into friendship and relationship with Him is hard for me to comprehend. But it is nonetheless true. The Bible tells us that if we confess our sins to the fathering God that He will forgive us (1 John 1:9). Jesus' example in Scripture is truly amazing. As He hung on the cross, bleeding out our redemption in pain and agony, He cried, "Father, forgive them." Ultimate forgiveness is waiting for us, a new relationship with the fathering God found only through Jesus.

If you have never realized the forgiveness that comes from God, there is no time like the present. He is waiting with outstretched arms for you to turn and come back to Him. In Him there is complete forgiveness, no matter the crime. Before we can begin to forgive our sons we need to be forgiven ourselves, and that can happen right now in the incredible grace and mercy of the fathering God.

By looking at the model of our Father God, we can catch a glimpse of what living as forgiving fathers should be like. By listening to His voice of comfort and release, we can find a way to release our own sons through forgiveness. The next few pages of this chapter will walk you through some facets of forgiveness, helping you to understand how to put the power of forgiveness to work in your relationship.

Forgiveness Is . . .

Forgiveness is first of all a canceling of a debt. When someone has hurt us, cheated us, or wronged us, he owes us. It is very much like a credit card. When we are wronged, we ring up a charge against that person, holding him to it until he pays it off. Forgiveness is marking the bill "paid in full." It means that we no longer hold our sons to their debt. We have pulled out their account and scribbled in large letters across the top, "Paid In Full." And then we tear up the account sheet and throw it away.

Your son will hurt you. I can guarantee it. Once in a fit of uncontrollable rage, I screamed at my father, "I hate you, and I'll always hate you!" Even though I was angry I regretted those words the moment they left my lips. But it was too late. My dad looked at me, his face pale, then turned his back on me and walked away. I followed him into his study. "Dad, I, I'm sorry, I . . . ." My voice trailed off because words weren't enough. The wound was deep. He waited for what seemed like eternity, turned back to me, and said, "It's all right. Forget about it. I love you. You are forgiven. Go to bed and get some rest."

What an incredible release! I couldn't believe he had already forgiven me. I knew that his hurt was still there, but I also could see written plainly across his face, "You owe me nothing. Account paid in full."

Forgiveness can be defined as the canceling of a debt, but it is more than debt. It is possible to cancel a debt and then remind a person the rest of his life how generous you were in canceling that debt. To forgive someone is also to release him, to give up any claim you have on him because of the wrong he has done you. To forgive your son is to pardon him without demanding any restitution, freeing him to live the rest of his life.

In forgiving our sons we are really setting them free from the tyranny of guilt and the manipulation that too often accompanies it. We also are freeing ourselves from the tyranny of our self-pity and grudges. We are letting go of the hurt and the pain even as we forgive.

Forgiveness is not dependent on a plea for redemption. If we wait for our sons to come to us and ask for forgiveness, we are placing the burden on the wrong shoulders. We bear the burden of forgiveness, not them. It is possible for us to forgive them even if they never realize they have caused us pain, or if they have realized it and don't care. True forgiveness is not dependent on our son's state of mind, his "remorse," or anything but our willingness to let it go, to release him.

Don't waste your life waiting for an apology that may never come. In waiting, fathers can become consumed by bitterness, and the love that they treasured is eaten away until there is nothing but emptiness left.

When you and I forgive our sons we are standing the world on end. We are putting our relationship with our sons above our feelings of justice and fairness. We are putting our love for our sons on trial, and with forgiveness we prove that love to be true and deep.

Forgiveness in a father-son relationship can be tricky business. Usually the fault for wounding each other isn't clear-cut. It is shared by you and your son, sometimes equally, more often not equally. Figuring out who is most wrong and should be most sorry is not forgiving but futile. Our relationships as fathers need to be characterized by a constant examining of ourselves to see where we have hurt our sons, a seeking of forgiveness for that hurt, and a generous spirit of forgiving our sons when they hurt us, releasing them, canceling the obligation, freeing them to live their lives.

Our relationship with our Father God is characterized by three stages. Often we are in all three at the same time. They are sin, grace, and forgiveness. Our fathering needs to be characterized the same way. Our sons need to feel their sin, to wash in our grace, and to live free in our forgiveness. By doing this we create an atmosphere that will supercharge our relationships. Past wrongs and hurts won't complicate our life. We will start each day with our sons with a clean slate, a spotless record. And then when sin enters our relationship, we can share the grace given us by the fathering God with our sons and let them feel the forgiveness that has come to us through Him.

Perhaps my favorite story in the Bible is when Peter asked Jesus how much forgiveness was enough. The conventional wisdom of his day was that forgiving someone three times was very generous and probably more than he deserved. Peter thought that he would go the extra mile and really impress his Master. "Jesus, how many times should I forgive someone? Seven times?" I can imagine Peter feeling a little smug as he uttered those words, more than doubling the conventional number of times. Surely he was being more than generous. Then Jesus turned Peter's (and our) world upside down with His idea of generosity in forgiveness. "Not seven times, but seventy times seven."

In a world that counts wrong and adds up debts, Jesus' words are revolutionary and earthshaking, but they are also the most comforting words I can imagine. Forgiveness from the Father God is limitless, flowing out of His unceasing grace and mercy. And the forgiveness we give to our sons needs to be just as limitless. To steal the ending from another great story, when our prodigal returns, we should meet him in the driveway, our smiles and tears of joy painting a clear picture: "Debt paid in full." Then we break out the good stuff and throw a party of unlimited forgiveness.

A Personal Story

At eighteen years old I was an angry young man. I was foundering in my faith, unsure of what I believed, and even less sure of what I wanted to do with my life. My fear and frustration often came out in angry words, in fits of rage. One evening I lost control during a discussion with my father. I don't even remember what the discussion was about. All I know is that I went from rational to totally

162

out of control in a few seconds. Being a verbal person, I began to insult my father. He ignored me and I became, if this was possible, even angrier at him. I hurled an epithet across our living room that had never been uttered in our house before or since. It was both unspeakably vulgar and cruel. Before I could even react my father, former hoodlum and bar brawler, had crossed the room and knocked me to the floor. As I lay on the floor looking up at my father, who stood there, chest heaving, fists clenched in rage, I couldn't let it go. "Did that make you feel like a big man?" I taunted him from the living room floor. "Why don't you kick me while I lie here? Would that make you feel tougher?" He looked hard at me, turned away, and left the room. I climbed to my feet and headed out the door.

An hour later I was back in the living room. I was still angry, but I was also ashamed. I knew that I had lost it. I knew I was wrong. I knew I had hurt my father, my friend. But I didn't know what to do about it. I didn't know how to say I was sorry, how to ask for forgiveness. I heard footsteps and turned as my dad entered the room. He stood facing me, and I waited for him to tell me that I had blown it, that he was profoundly disappointed in me, that I had ruined our relationship. But he simply looked at me and said quietly, "Jack, I'm sorry I lost my temper and threw you to the ground. I was wrong. I'm sorry I blew it. Forgive me." With that he turned and walked back out of the room.

I couldn't believe my ears. No "I was wrong but you were more wrong." Or even, "You deserved what you got, boy. Think before you talk next time." Simply, "I'm sorry. Forgive me." It slowly dawned on me that my father had already forgiven me, had already let go of the pain and the hurt I had brought into his life. He was seeking my forgiveness to bring the issue to a close, and he wasn't waiting for an apology from me that I didn't have the strength of character to deliver.

I learned that day how to ask for forgiveness. I learned how to apologize. I learned what it felt like to be forgiven. But most important of all, on that day I began to understand what it means to be a man.

How Forgiving Are You?

Please respond to the statements below using the following scale to help you measure forgiveness in your life.

1 = Almost never   4 = Frequently
2 = Once in a while   5 = Almost always
3 = Sometimes

_____ 1. It is hard for me to forgive those who hurt me.

_____ 2. I am able to forget my mistakes and failures.

_____ 3. It is hard for me to forgive myself for things I have done.

_____ 4. I believe that when people say they forgive me they really mean it.

_____ 5. It is hard for me to admit that I am wrong.

_____ 6. I sense very strongly that I am completely forgiven by God.

_____ 7. I find myself thinking about getting even with those who hurt me.

_____ 8. I am able to forget past offenses against me.

_____ 9. I get angry at myself for the stupid things I do.

_____ 10. I find it easy to forgive those who offend me.

_____ 11. I tend to hold grudges against others.

_____ 12. I am able to forgive those who hurt someone I love.

Describe yourself as a forgiving person: (check one in each column)

Forgiving Others
___ very forgiving of others
___ usually forgiving of others
___ somewhat forgiving of others
___ struggle to forgive others
___ unforgiving of others

Forgiving Self
___ very forgiving of self
___ usually forgiving of self
___ somewhat forgiving of self
___ struggle to forgive self
___ unforgiving of self

Optional: Have someone close to you (spouse, friend, or son) take this forgiveness scale and rate you. Compare their rating to your own. Talk about it with them.

Chapter Twelve

Building on the Rock

...the fathering strength of spiritual wellness

Doug Vande Guchte and his three sons, Tim, twenty-five, Todd, twenty-three, and Tyler, nineteen, share one thing in common. It's not what they do for a living, although as a construction engineer with three painter sons they do share some similarities there. What they have in common is a love for Jesus. And on that very solid foundation they have based their remarkable relationship.

Doug Vande Guchte and his sons have succeeded where so many others have fallen short. They have developed a relationship not just with each other but with the fathering God as well. We asked the Vande Guchtes what has made their relationships what they are today.

"God. A simple answer, but it's the truth. The relationship we were taught to have with Christ, while living in this home, through family devotions, through prayer, or just through discussions and talking about it."

"I think of the times we spent together as a family around this table eating dinner, and always starting out dinner thanking God for all that He had blessed us with, or even the food we were able to eat. And I remember the close of dinner. We spent time praying and reading the Bible. As a junior high kid the last thing you want to do is sit for another ten or fifteen minutes around the dinner table with your parents. You want to eat your food and run out the door. I think it took a lot of diligence and dedication for Dad to say, 'This is best, and tonight we're going to read from God's Word even if you don't really want to.' "

"To think of doing that not just for one or even two years, but year after year, being willing to spend time praying and showing us who our God is and how much He's done for us. I look back now and think, *That was one of the major pluses, the major positives in our life together.*"

Spiritual Wellness?

Spiritual wellness is not a New Age term or an attempt to water down our faith. Nor does it simply mean a family who calls themselves Christians. Spiritual wellness in a family means a living and vital Christianity that results in both the fathers and sons feeling at peace with each other and with their Father God. A spiritually well family takes their faith seriously and lets it impact their lives. It is not enough for them to go to church and then leave their faith on the front porch of their home until next Sunday. Spiritually well fathers and sons make God an intimate part of their everyday lives. They invite Jesus into their parenting, into their activities together, into their disagreements, and into their difficulties. They can't imagine getting through the day without help from their fathering God.

The Vande Guchtes explain, "This family wouldn't be what it is apart from God, and I think that has infiltrated and affected every decision that we've made as a family and impacted the relationships we have. We can't leave God out of the picture. God is everything to us. He is life, and that's what caused my grandpa to be who he was, and my father to be who he is."

Using a definition we've adapted from noted Christian counselor Gary Collins, spiritual wellness is a sense of being at peace with the Father God, understanding our place in His plan and His love for us and our sons. It is not something we possess; it is a gift from God to us and our sons. To be spiritually well is to understand that God loves, accepts, and forgives us and that He asks us to follow

166

Him every day. Spiritual wellness is exhibited through the fruit of the Spirit of God in our lives. Paul writes in Galatians 5, "But the fruit of the spirit is love, joy, peace, patience, kindness, goodness, faithfulness, gentleness, and self-control. Against such things there is no law" (vv. 22-23).

When we begin to exhibit these qualities in our life and in our relationship with our sons, we are truly on the way to a profound and rewarding friendship with them. The character the Spirit of God is building in our lives affects all that we do, but it is especially seen in our relationships with others. And if we want a lifelong friendship with our sons, gentleness, patience, kindness, self-control, and faithfulness will be the foundation we build that relationship on.

What Does Spiritual Wellness Bring to Our Relationship with Our Sons?

When we build spiritual wellness into our lives, we are declaring what we stand for as a family. More than anything else, this strength defines what we are all about. Spiritually well fathers and sons know that they are first and foremost about doing God's work and will and that everything else — money, power, prestige, possessions — doesn't matter in the long run.

I remember when I was young a boy and my father was in his first pastorate. We were driving toward Chicago; the sun was shining, and it was a good day to be out with my dad. We weren't talking about anything important when my father suddenly got a serious look on his face, turned to me, and said, "Jackson, whatever else happens to you in this life, nothing matters except being faithful to God. No matter what happens, be faithful." I didn't have the foggiest idea what he was talking about, but he was my dad and I loved him. So I smiled and nodded my head. Little did I know that I would hear those words for the rest of my life.

When I entered high school my dad took me aside. "No matter what, Jack, it all comes down to being faithful to Jesus." When I graduated from high school: "I'm proud of you, Jack. Keep on being faithful to God. Nothing else matters." When I got married his advice was the same, and when I began my ministry as a youth pastor and things didn't exactly go the way I wanted them to go, his words came back to me. "Be faithful, Jack. That is all you can do. Be faithful to God's call on your life."

Those words were what we lived by. They defined our family. They gave us a purpose for everything we did. The first time my father spoke those words to me, he wasn't a pastor at one of the largest churches in the state. He wasn't a well-known speaker. He wasn't the author of three books. He was the pastor of a tiny, inner-city church that could barely afford to pay him. But it didn't matter. Our family was defined by our faithfulness to God's call.

That is what spiritual wellness did for us. It gave us a purpose and a reason for existence. It gave my brother and me a reason to do our best in life and eventually to give our lives to the fathering God. It can do the same thing in your family. Building the strength of spiritual wellness into your fathering will give your fathering a purpose it may have lacked before.

Even more, you will provide a base of shared values for you and your sons. Spiritual wellness provides our fathering with purpose, but it also gives us a way to explain and pass on our values to our sons. "We are followers of Jesus in this family, and therefore we help the needy, and give of our time to the church, and pray and read the Bible." What many fathers and sons lack today is precisely what comes through spiritual wellness — a shared, common set of values.

This is perhaps the most important thing to fathers: that our children grow up and live out the values and faith that are the building blocks of our life. We want our kids to care about what we care about, to believe what we believe, to see right and wrong the way we see right and wrong. The best way to achieve this is through the strength of spiritual wellness.

My father and I have disagreed over many things, perhaps none more strongly than politics. Dad is a conservative Republican and proud of it. What's more, he is quite sure that anyone who has thought about the issues will be a conservative Republican too. I came back after two trips to the Third World with different ideas. We talked, and discussed, and argued, and made fun of each other's ideas, and then laughed at ourselves until we cried. But even though we vote for different people, our values are still basically the same. We just differ over how to achieve them. That has enabled my dad to put up with a lot of rather dumb ideas from me without blowing his top. He knows that we share the same core values and that eventually I'm going to come down to earth again.

Through the strength of spiritual wellness my dad and I are almost always on the same page regarding what is important to us and what really matters, even if we differ on how to achieve those goals. More than anything else, the reason my dad and I have the relationship we share today is because of the spiritual wellness in our relationship. Without it we would not be writing this book; we would not share the friendship that brings so much joy to our lives.

How Do We Build Spiritual Wellness?

Pastor Dan Cummings has thought long and hard about this issue. More than anything he desperately wants his sons to follow him in the faith. When we interviewed him he spent a lot of time talking about Christianity and how tough it can be today to pass along one's faith and values, to find a true Christianity, to build spiritual wellness into a fathering relationship.

"My pilgrimage has been to find out what are the essential things and to anchor into them, grabbing all the help I can along the way. What are the essential things? The essential things seem to be, 'Cummings, live the way Jesus would live with your sons, and don't forget to live with them.' "

Dan has caught the tough truth of building spiritual wellness, a living relationship with the Father God, into our fathering: there aren't ten steps or five ways to make it easier. Building spiritual wellness into our lives means *cultivating a living and vital relationship with the Creator.* That seems obvious, but it is so central to fathering that it cannot be overemphasized. If we want Jesus present in our fathering and present in our sons, then He must be present in our lives first. It doesn't work to preach it without living it. All of us have to pay more attention to our spiritual lives. All of us have to make our relationship with the fathering God a priority or our sons never will. I fear that too many times I talk the holy talk but fail to walk the holy walk. I know that my son is watching me and that he is learning what it means to be a follower of Jesus from me. That scares me, but it also drives me to take my relationship with the Father God seriously. Jonathon's watchful gaze provides an impetus to cultivate and nurture God's presence in my life.

Our challenge to you is to do the same. If you want to build a strong relationship with your son, the foundation that never crumbles is the fathering God. Make getting to know Him and building the fathering strength of spiritual wellness the first priority in your life. No shortcuts here. Knowing God requires discipline and some work, but it is worth it.

We won't take much time here to talk about how to build a relationship with God. Many great books have been written on the subject, and your Christian bookstore is full of books that will encourage you and inspire you in your journey to the Father God. But we do want to say two things. First, in our interviews with fathers and sons we found out that the Scriptures are right: The fervent prayer of a righteous man does avail much (James 5:16). These fathers and sons spoke often and eloquently about the role prayer has played in their lives. Sons spoke of how they learned about God from the prayers of their fathers. Fathers spoke of crying out to God in prayer for help when fathering their sons became difficult or when their sons turned away from them. Whatever else getting to know God involves, it will involve prayer.

Second, the fathers and sons we talked to spoke often of the Bible and the guidance that God's Word had provided for them. Sons told of seeing their fathers with open Bibles seeking to know God more and to understand Him better. Fathers told of praying the Psalms during difficult times and reading Jesus' words of comfort and joy. If prayer is a prerequisite to getting to know God, so is reading the Bible, God's Word.

Spiritual wellness is also *a gift from the Father God that comes through His grace.* While we must nurture and cultivate this relationship, we must realize that it doesn't originate with us or happen because of what we do or don't do. God's presence in our lives is a gift from Him, and His presence in our fathering is a gift from Him. No formula will make it happen; no incantation will guarantee that spiritual wellness will become a part of our lives. It is God's grace being made real to us when He enters into relationship with us. It is God's grace and mercy that we first sense when our sons choose to take advantage of His rich gift.

Never lose sight of the fact that God comes into our lives because He loves us and wants to be in relationship with us. That means He wants to be in relationship with our sons and wants to be a part of our relationship as fathers and sons. He is the Father God, and we as fathers matter to Him.

As we attempt to build spiritual wellness into our lives, *we need to realize that shared values and faith do not mean identical values and faith.* Our sons don't have to cross every *t* and dot every *i* exactly the way we do. If we insist on a legalistic, narrow Christianity that demands our sons believe everything exactly the same way expressed in the same words and worshiped in the same form as we do, we will drive our sons away from God and spiritual wellness out of our lives.

To share values doesn't mean that our sons must perfectly duplicate every value we have. It means that the same things matter to us; we hold the same things to be important. We value and believe in the same things, though we may often express those values and beliefs differently.

My father is one of the pastors at Calvary Church in Grand Rapids, Michigan. Calvary is a huge church with thousands of people in its multiple worship services. It is also a fairly conservative church in its worship style. I love Calvary Church, but I like Covenant Life more.

Covenant Life Church in the small resort town of Grand Haven, Michigan, counts its attendance in the hundreds, not the thousands, and our meeting place is a partially renovated warehouse in the center city district, just off the waterfront. Our worship style is more liturgical than Calvary's, our music more contemporary. I like being a pastor at Covenant Life.

My brother likes Calvary, and he thinks Covenant Life has a

171

cool building, but he likes Hope Reformed. He likes the family atmosphere and the reformed tradition. He likes the slower pace at his church and wouldn't trade it for anything.

All of us go to church. All of us value worship. All of us worship differently. My father could get angry with me or my brother and say, "Why don't you like Calvary? Why don't you come to my church and do things my way?" But he knows better. We share the same value — church attendance — but we express it in different ways.

Fathers who want to build spiritual wellness into their families need to let their sons explore God and His world in their own way. We need to let God speak to our sons through their personalities and gifts, likes and dislikes. And we need to know that a little diversity promotes spiritual growth and brings all of us, fathers and sons, closer to the Father God.

Last, it is most important to realize that *spiritual wellness is caught much more often than it is taught.* Sitting down with your son and lecturing to him about God isn't necessarily bad. Living every day of your life as a follower of Jesus is much better. I learned much more by watching my father as he loved my mother, as he ministered to his congregation, as he loved his friends, and as he lived his life as if it mattered, than I ever did from his sermons.

One image of my father sticks with me from my youth. I was only about nine years old when Dad took me to downtown Chicago to the Pacific Garden Mission. I had never been to a mission before, and I was scared to death. The place was filled with smelly, filthy, loud men, people I had never been in contact with before. In my sanitized world there were good people. They had jobs, took baths, got married, and went to church. And there were bad people. They lived on the street, drank alcohol, smoked cigarettes, didn't have jobs, and never went to church. Such is the mind of a nine-year-old. These men were so bad according to my calculations that they were off the scale. I don't remember much of what happened that evening. I just have an image of my dad with his arm around a lice-infested man who reeked of liquor and garbage, telling him that Jesus loved him. My sanitized version of the world was knocked completely out of whack. There was my clean-cut pastor father, touching a "bad" man.

I learned a lot about Jesus that night. I learned a lot about the Gospel. I learned a lot about forgiveness. And I learned a lot about my father. On that night I caught the bug of spiritual wellness from my dad. I still haven't gotten over it, and our relationship has been greatly enhanced by it.

Deuteronomy may seem like an odd place for advice on a contemporary topic like fathering sons and spiritual wellness. But in chapter 6 of this book of the Law, God's commands to Israel sum up the principle of spiritual wellness completely:

"Hear, O Israel: The Lord our God, the Lord is one. Love the Lord your God with all your heart and with all your soul and with all your strength. These commandments that I give to you today are to be upon your hearts. Impress them on your children. Talk about them when you sit at home and when you walk along the road, when you lie down and when you get up. Tie them as symbols on your hands and bind them on your foreheads. Write them on the door frames of your houses and your gates." (Deuteronomy 6:4-9)

The lawgiver understood that loving God and responding to His love and grace is an all-encompassing endeavor. Building spiritual wellness into your family is the same. It means that we must live our lives with a difference. We father with a difference. We go to our jobs and to our play with a difference because we belong to the Father God. He has called us His sons, and we will never be the same again.

It is my prayer that God's commandments will be written large on the door frames of my house, that all who enter will know they are entering a home that is first and foremost God's. I also hope that these commandments will be on the lips of my son as he goes through life. I pray that he will love Jesus and will begin to understand the grace that God has bestowed on his life. I hope and pray more than anything that he will live his life in relationship to the Father God, that he will accept God's free gift of salvation through Jesus Christ. And I hope that I can a be part of leading him there, and that our relationship will be characterized by a shared love for the Father God and His Son, Jesus Christ, just as my relationship with my father has been.

We pray that you too will build this strength into your life, realizing that ultimately it is God who comes to us and calls us and our sons to Himself. But remember that we must cultivate our own relationship with God. Understand that our sons can follow Jesus in their way, not just our way, and that ultimately how we live is a much more accurate judge of our lives and our relationship with God than how we talk.

Twelve Activities to Build Spiritual Wellness

The following activities are suggestions to help you develop the spiritual aspect of your relationship with your son. Some are more appropriate for certain ages. Choose two or three and grow together.

1. Take your son with you on a missions trip to the Third World or the inner city.
2. Read through the Bible with your son.
3. Have devotions together on a hike through the woods, by a stream, in the mountains, alongside a lake.
4. Experience a "coming of age" retreat with your son. This could be as simple as a dinner together, or a weekend away. Explain what it means to be "man of God." Encourage him toward that.
5. Work together one day a week or month in an inner-city ministry such as a soup kitchen or homeless shelter.
6. Be alert to teachable moments throughout the day to relate spiritual truths.
7. Keep a journal and share with your son periodically. Have him do the same.
8. Do something special together for your son's mother.
9. Develop a "partners in prayer" list. Pray for his friends and his concerns. Have him do the same for you.
10. Support a missionary together, write letter to him or her, even visit the missionary together.
11. Discuss the pastor's message after church regularly. Find out what your son is hearing and learning.
12. Worship together, sing songs, pray, be silent together, go to church together. Fill your life together with worship.

Chapter Thirteen

Closer Than a Brother

...the fathering strength of cohesion

"I guess one of the ways that I can describe what it was like growing up with my dad is when I was in junior high and wrote a paper on who my hero was or who I looked up to. As a kid you always have sports heroes, people you look up to that you think are really cool. But when I thought about who I looked up to the most, well, I always looked up to my dad. He was my hero."

Greg Ohlman

"Being a school teacher has helped me develop a close relationship with my sons. During the summers we'd take time to go on long vacations, camping across the country. Those long trips would bring out the worst and the best in us, and when things weren't good we had to sit down and hammer them out. There were a lot of neat opportunities to explore together, to hike and camp in the mountains. It was good to be together."

Jerry Southland

"I think one of the things that has helped us to be as close as we are is that I've really taken the time to be available. There's a lot of pursuits, a lot of challenges with your marriage, your own special interests and hobbies. I guess I've made it a point to be home, to be with my sons. It's a lot of little decisions really.

Somebody asks, 'Do you want to play in this league?' or, 'Do you want to work late on this project?' And I just got in the habit of saying no."

Vic Forester

"I did my stint during the night, feeding them and changing them when they were babies. I got up at 2:00 A.M. and looked forward to it as much as I looked forward to the nights that I would sleep. We would take turns — one night mine, one night was my wife's. Then it kind of evolved from there and we'd just do stuff as a family. We did everything together. Our kids' friends would call up on a weekend and say, 'Do you want to do this?' or, 'Do you want to go here?' And the answer usually was, 'Well, my mom and dad and I are going to go here and there this weekend.' "

Doug Lapinski

"One of the things that has really drawn my sons and me together was when about ten or twelve years ago I was diagnosed as having multiple sclerosis. Mary and I came home from the doctors and told the family. We had sort of a family meeting, a pretty emotional, scary type meeting. But we felt the commitment on the part of the kids, that they were there for me. That has been a real key element in our being very cohesive as a family."

Jim Dice

All of these families come from different economic and social backgrounds. They have different ways of building their father-son relationship. But they all share one common characteristic: all of the fathers and sons you heard from exhibit the fathering strength of cohesion.

Cohesion means emotional closeness. A cohesive father and son have forged an emotional bond that transcends circumstances and petty disagreements. Cohesive fathers and sons feel close to one another emotionally. They trust each other and depend on each other.

Cohesion is not a fathering strength that is built like most of the others. You don't wake up one morning and say, "We're going to

176

be a more cohesive family today. We're going to feel emotionally close, even if it kills us!" Cohesion doesn't work that way. It is a product of the other fathering strengths. It comes out of them and then enhances and helps build them even stronger. Cohesion is a product of many different actions, attitudes, and activities. It won't happen in your family overnight, but once it is built, that emotional closeness encourages activities and attitudes that keep building cohesion. Once it reaches a critical mass, cohesion in your father-son relationship becomes an enormous asset in your life. It makes every experience with your son richer. It takes your best talks with him deeper, and it pushes you to spend time with him.

HI and LOIS ®   **By Mort Walker & Dik Browne**

WHAT A GOOD HUGGER! NOW DADDY NEEDS A HUG

OH, TRIXIE NEEDS A HUG, TOO

WHAT'S WRONG, CHIP?

I HATE TO ADMIT IT, BUT I THINK I NEED A HUG, TOO!

BROWNE 7-2

Reprinted with special permission of King Features Syndicate.

This fathering strength is really about what we want most from our relationships with our sons. Cohesion is all about the friendship that we forge with them. It is all about trusting our sons to stand by us during difficult times, and their knowing that we will be there for them. A cohesive relationship between father and son provides us with enormous security and safety. Cohesion is the glue that holds us together when everything else is falling apart. It makes loyalty and trust possible, late-night talks with your dad so fulfilling, and early morning runs with your son so full of joy. This is why we father, because we want to feel emotionally close to our sons.

We've already given you some examples of what cohesion looks like in a family through the quotes from the fathers and sons that opened the chapter. You may have found yourself nodding your head as you read those quotes, understanding exactly what they were talking about and recognizing your own relationship in their statements. Or you may have shook your head, realizing that your relationship with your son is not what it ought to be, not characterized by emotional closeness. Our advice to you again is don't give up. In this chapter we will show you the five marks of a cohesive family and then show how the other fathering strengths build cohesion, emotional closeness, into a relationship. By the time you turn the last page of this chapter, you will know exactly how to continue or start growing your son closer to you and building emotional closeness into your relationship.

The Five Marks of a Cohesive Relationship

How do you know if you are building cohesion in your relationship with your son? Through our research and the research of many others, we have been able to identify five marks of a cohesive relationship. Now realize that every father and son who are emotionally close don't necessarily exhibit every one of these marks every day of their lives. Sometimes we are closer together and all of these characteristics apply to us; sometimes we have drifted apart for a time and they are not as prevalent in our life. Don't get hung up on the fact that you and your son only exhibit three or four of the marks of a cohesive relationship. Having three or four is pretty good, and having all five all the time is tough to do.

As you read through these characteristics, ask yourself some questions. Are my son and I doing this? Does this characterize our relationship? What could we do to build more of this in our life? Are we moving toward these goals or away from them? Get personally involved in this chapter, and find out how you are doing in growing emotional closeness.

1. Fathers and sons ask each other for help. My father loves electronics. He likes gadgets and gee-whiz technology. The problem is that electronics don't like him. He has an almost uncanny ability to cause a working piece of equipment to stop working.

Bring my father near an automobile and he will make it hum, but stand him next to a computer and it is bound to crash. That doesn't stop Dad, however. He doesn't take our computer's rejection of him personally. He keeps coming back for more. Today he tried to hook up the fax modem in our notebook computer so I could fax him this chapter. It didn't work. Never mind that yesterday when I had the notebook the fax modem worked fine. For my father it rebelled. Not only that, while he fiddled with the fax modem somehow the hard drive began to complain. So my phone rang. "Jack, I'm having a little trouble with the notebook. . . ."

It was not the first time he has called me for computer help, and I can guarantee it won't be the last. We never did get the fax modem working, but his call to me for help underscored how close we have become emotionally. That phone call and the hundreds like it between my dad and me are a mark of our cohesiveness.

Cohesive fathers and sons are not afraid to ask each other for help. They are so close emotionally that they don't worry about little things like pride, and who is older, and who should have all the answers. Cohesive fathers and sons look to each other for help and guidance, and they do it regularly and often without thinking. It is natural for them. I've been in ministry for ten years, while my dad has been in ministry in one way or another for almost thirty years. So it is natural for me to call my dad when I'm dealing with a problem in my church. He knows more than I do, and I ask him for his help in my pastoring nearly every week.

I was talking to another pastor friend of mine about this not long ago. His father had been a pastor as well, and we had joked many times about being "PKs" and about subjecting our own children to that distinction. The difference between my friend and me is that his father was authoritarian and judgmental. When I casually mentioned that I asked my father for help on a weekly basis, he just shook his head. "I could never do that, Jack. I've spent so many years trying to get out of his shadow and beyond his reach. To ask him for help would just give him power over me again."

I don't understand my friend's problem very well, because my father has never taken my requests for help as an opportunity to make himself look good or to lord his knowledge over me. Instead, he has acted as if it were a privilege to help me and as if I were doing him a favor by letting him help me. It is a measure of our relationship that we ask each other without fear and without any power plays.

I want to strongly encourage you to build this into your relationship with your son. Helping our sons is easy when they are young. They ask us all the time for help; in fact, sometimes it seems their requests are unending. But as they grow and mature it becomes more difficult for them to ask us for help. They are trying to establish their own identity apart from us, and looking to us for help is not easy — which is precisely the reason when they *do* turn to us we need to treat their requests with great respect and dignity, and we need to honor that request for help.

Many men have trouble admitting to their sons that they don't have all the answers and that they need their sons' help. Get over your pride and let your son help you. It will draw you closer together and strengthen your relationship. Forget about the fact that "father knows best" and ask away. Let your son see that you respect him by asking him questions, by coming to him for some answers, and by letting him know that you value his opinion.

I'll never forget the first time my minister-father asked for my advice on a ministry matter. Now understand that my dad is a good pastor and a great teacher. His ministry skills are terrific, and I have spent the last ten years learning from him. But a few years ago my dad came to me and asked for my advice on an issue I thought he knew more about than I. "Jack, you have a way with teenagers, and I love the way you speak to them. I'm doing a chapel at the Christian school this week, and I'm wondering if you could give me some advice." "What kind of advice, Dad? What do you mean?" "Well, could you give me a couple of pointers on speaking to teens? It's been a long time since I've spoken to high school students, and any advice or tips you might have would be very welcome."

Do you see how asking for help both shows how close a relationship is and also helps build a relationship stronger? By asking me for help, my dad managed to affirm me, to show me that he trusted and respected me and my abilities, and that he considered me an equal. I was floored. It was enormously important to me, ranking only slightly below the first time I beat him in Ping-Pong in importance on my developmental scale.

Ask for help and give your help when asked. Your ability to do those things indicates how close your relationship with your son truly is. If he is coming to you for help or advice, he feels safe with you and secure enough to show that he doesn't have it all together. If you can go to him for help, you are showing him exactly how much you value him.

2. *Fathers and sons spend free time together.* We have talked about this in other places in this book but it needs to be said again. If you are close emotionally with your son, you will want to spend time together. You won't schedule your life so full that you don't have time to be together to do the things you like to do. If your son feels close to you, he will include you in his life. That doesn't necessarily mean that he will want to be with you every time you want to be with him, or that he won't want to be with his friends. It does mean that he will make the effort to spend time with you and that you will do the same.

I hear so many dads tell me that they are close to their sons, but they don't spend their free time with them. Instead, they play golf three times a week with their buddies, or they go fishing with their friends, or they indulge in any number of good things to do. Then when their sons are gone from home and they never call, these same fathers wonder why. Close fathers and sons make being together a priority.

Dan Cummings is an avid golfer, and he's pretty good at it as well. He has a membership at one of the best courses near his home. But does he play on Saturday morings with his buddies? No. Dan takes that time to be with his sons. "I love to golf," he says, "so Benjamin rides in the cart and chases squirrels out at the club. He likes to take the flag in and out, and he rakes the sand traps for me. I don't go golfing on Saturday morings. I go on Tuesday morning when nobody is out there and no one cares if a little kid is raking the traps and chasing squirrels."

3. *Fathers and sons consult each other on decisions.* I bought a

car four years ago without talking to my dad about it. It was the worst car I ever owned. It spent more time in my garage than out on the road. I finally got rid of it, taking a beating on the price. I should have asked my dad about buying it, because he would have warned me off. I haven't bought another car since without first asking his advice.

My brother just bought a new house. He agonized for a while over which house to buy. There were two homes that met all of his criteria. He took my dad through each home and then asked for his honest opinion. "I like the one on Oakwood, Jon, and here's why. . . ." My brother talked it over with his wife, called and asked me, and decided my father was right. He bought the house on Oakwood.

We don't consult our father because we're afraid to make a move without his blessing. We don't ask his advice because we are codependent and unable to make a decision unless he signs off on it first. We consult my dad on major decisions because we respect him and his opinion, and we believe that he has our best interests at heart. He is one of our best friends, and it makes sense to ask him what he thinks.

Cohesive fathers and sons consult with each other before making major decisions. Don't misunderstand this. They don't have to do this, and it is not a controlling gesture. They want to share the decision with the people they feel closest to, so they tell their dads and the dads tell their sons. Nathan Hillman is a great example of this. Nathan is an accomplished student, very bright and articulate, but he consults with his dad on most major decisions. He doesn't have to; he wants to. "During my third year at college our communication deepened," Nathan says. "I was deeply in love with a woman. My world began to crumble as she pulled away, but I heard my father's voice (over e-mail most of the time), a voice filling my empty pit of loss." Nathan goes on to describe how more than one girl has mentioned in frustration to him, "You're too close to your dad. It's like he stands between us." Nathan realizes that is a danger, but he loves his father and feels very close to him and plans to continue to consult him about decisions.

Of course, consulting works the other way as well, with fathers consulting their sons before making a decision. I was speaking last week with a father who was contemplating a job change. He told me, "I would never take such a big step without talking to my son. He is so level-headed and such a clear thinker. I really value his opinion."

4. *Fathers and sons want to build "togetherness."* Every relationship is complex, consisting of alternating needs and wants that change and grow, sometimes quickly, sometimes not. Sometimes a relationship needs space and separateness, but more often a relationship requires more "togetherness." Cohesive fathers and sons constantly try to find new ways to grow closer, to build that elusive togetherness through a variety of shared thoughts and experiences. The families we have identified as cohesive have built this togetherness in a diverse manner. Some of them have done it in the mountains, some in their backyards, some through their faith, some through a trip to the movies. The possibilities are endless, but if you are a cohesive father and son you will actively find ways to build togetherness.

One of the primary ways my father and I build togetherness is by traveling together. We travel often to speak together, and while on those trips we always try to explore the place we are visiting, whether it is Kauai, Hawaii or Hamilton, Ontario. Those trips build togetherness in our lives.

Togetherness is built by doing things with other family members and by doing things with just the two of you. There needs to be a balance between those two methods. Too much of just the two of you and you will feel isolated. Too much of being with others and you won't have the opportunity to build special "just you and me" moments.

5. *Fathers and sons feel close to each other and value that feeling.* The final mark of cohesion is almost self-evident. Cohesive fathers and sons feel close to each other. They feel connected and in touch. They feel like they know each other and understand each other. They value that feeling, and when it goes away they seek to restore it, to rebuild the closeness that has been lost. Fathers and sons who have enjoyed cohesion miss it when it is no longer there and they want it back.

Look at your relationship with your son. Do you feel close to him? Don't worry about whether you've been angry at him or if you've had a fight. That happens, but do you feel connected with him? Do you think he feels connected with you? Would you realize it if you were no longer that close? Would you be able to feel the distance between you? Those are the questions you need to answer as you seek to discover the level of cohesion in your father-son relationship.

Ten Ways to Build Cohesion

At the beginning of this chapter I mentioned that cohesion is built by the other fathering strengths. That is why this is the last chapter examining those strengths. Cohesiveness doesn't happen overnight. As you and your son develop the other fathering strengths, cohesion will be a natural product. It doesn't come of its own accord. Here are ten ways to build cohesion into your life.

1. *Play and laugh together.*
2. *Deal with conflict effectively and positively.*
3. *Affirm and appreciate each other.*
4. *Spend vast quantities of time together.*
5. *Be adaptable.*
6. *Forgive each other.*
7. *Worship together.*
8. *Trust and respect each other.*
9. *Help each other be all you can be.*
10. *Communicate positively.*

Cohesion is not a negative dependence. It is realizing that all of us need someone, and for close fathers and sons it means realizing that we have found that someone in each other. It means that we can rest in each other's presence, knowing that we are accepted and loved. We know that someone is on our side, believes in us, and wants the best for us. We know that we have a friend who is closer than a brother, who will stand by us loyally whatever comes. It means we have that rarest of people in our lives — a friend.

*Cohesion in Your Family**

Describe your relationship with your son. Use the following scale for your response.

1 = Almost never   4 = Frequently
2 = Once in a while   5 = Almost always
3 = Sometimes

_____ 1. We ask each other for help.

_____ 2. I approve of his friends.

_____ 3. We like to do things together.

_____ 4. We feel closer to each other than to people outside our family.

_____ 5. We like to spend free time together.

_____ 6. We feel very close to each other.

_____ 7. We share hobbies and interests together.

_____ 8. We can easily think of things to do together.

_____ 9. We consult each other on our deicions.

_____ 10. Togetherness is a top priority.

Scoring: Total your responses.
If your total is between 10 and 34, you are fairly disengaged from your son. For a closer relationship look at the items on which you scored three or below and try to practice them more frequently.
A score of 35-39 indicates low to moderate closeness;
40-44 moderate to high closeness;
45-50 very high closeness, high loyalty, and high dependency upon each other.

*Adapted from Circumplex Model of Marital and Family Systems, Dr. David Olson, University of Minnesota. Used by permission.

Chapter Fourteen

Our Father Who Is in Heaven

We have spent the better part of this book sharing fathering strengths, characteristics that strong fathers exhibit and use to build a friendship with their sons. You have met many different fathers from many different walks of life, and you have spent a lot of time getting to know our family. Perhaps the most important thing we have to say, however, will be said in the next few pages. You and I are not fathering our sons alone. Before we were ever fathers, before we were men, we were sons. Not just sons of our fathers, but all of us who name Jesus as Lord are sons of the same father, the Father God. And before we can be whole people and good fathers, we need to come to grips with what it means to be a child of the King.

It is possible that you haven't taken the time to get to know the Father God. You know God as creator and God as redeemer, but you've never explored the biblical portrait of God as our Father beyond using that title as a way to begin a prayer. In the next pages we want to introduce you to the God who fathers us. We will meet Him primarily through His Old Testament names. These names of God are far more important than our common names, such as, Jack, Jerry, Bill, and Sally. Our names do not convey much—if anything—about who we are or what we are like as persons. God's names are different, for they were used by the

writers of Scripture as descriptions of Him. They tell us what God
is like and how He fathers us; they reveal His character and His
promises to His people and tell us who He is.

Why is this important? Because so many people have been
fathered badly. In reading this book you may have laughed or
been filled with hope, but that father ache in your life, what
Gordon Dalbey so aptly calls our "father wound," threatens to
overtake you. You wonder how you can be the father you want to
be when your role model was so poor and your training in the
strengths nonexistent. In this chapter you will meet a role model
for you to emulate. You will find the Father who never lashes out,
never quits, and never gives up on you.

Perhaps you lay awake at night with an almost unending pain
inside. Whether your father was great or not doesn't seem to
matter; you are lonely and afraid as you try to father your son. In
these pages you will meet the Father God who sustains and uplifts
you, who will fill your empty soul with love and give you the
strength to be the father you want to be.

Ultimately, this is the most important chapter of this book
because we believe that good fathering of sons begins with being
good sons of the Father. Building a relationship to last a lifetime
with our sons happens best when we are in relationship to the One
who calls us children and who promises an unending legacy of
grace. Walk with us as we explore how God fathers us and in turn
inspires us to father our sons with grace and love.

Elohim: the Covenant-Keeping Father

God is named *Elohim* no fewer than 2,500 times in the Old
Testament, 32 times in the first chapter of Genesis alone. This
common name is special because it tells us about our uncommon
God. *Elohim* comes from two root words: *El*, signifying unlimited
strength and power, and *Alah*, meaning "to swear or make a
covenant." The meaning of *Elohim* then is "the God who promises
and has the might to keep His promises." Elohim is the God who
covenanted with Noah (Genesis 6:15-18) and the God who promised a son to elderly Abraham (Genesis 17:1-4). This God does not

make idle promises. When He covenants with us He has the means and the might to live up to His commitment. He is the promise-keeping Father. Other people will fail us. Our own fathers will fall short of their promises to us. They will quit and fail, but Elohim always keeps His word.

God has promised to never leave us or forsake us. When fathering our own sons seems to be too much, Elohim has promised He will not leave us. When we are caught between work and family, Elohim speaks softly to us, "Follow Me. Keep your word as I have kept Mine." Elohim serves us as both instructor and comforter. We learn from Elohim to follow through on our commitments to our families even when it is not easy. We learn from Elohim that our promises are important to our sons and that they must be honored. And we learn from Elohim that our fathering God will keep His promises to us, that He is the almighty keeper of His word. As the creator God, He is capable of doing what He has said He will do.

What an incredible example Elohim is for us. He is the strong, faithful Father. Living up to our commitments as men can be difficult in an age when commitments seem made to be broken. It can be hard to see the quick, thoughtless promise we made to our sons yesterday as binding today. It is possible that our own fathers failed to keep faith with us. You may have grown up with a father who walked out on you after promising to be there. Your image of a father may be a note and a check on Christmas or a wistful telephone call from a dad who never seems to be there. The good news is that Elohim is not that kind of father. He is the faithful One, and He will never break faith with us, His sons, called by His name. Elohim has made promises and He will keep them.

From Elohim we must learn that our promises are important. Our willingness to abandon our words signifies a deep breaking of faith with our sons. Our goal must be to emulate the faithful Father, who loves us from heaven. This generation of sons desperately needs fathers who are faithful to their word and to their promises. And perhaps the most amazing thing of all is that Elohim has covenanted with us to give us strength where we are weak, to become our courage when we are afraid, and to stiffen our resolve when we are ready to break faith. Elohim will help us become faithful fathers.

I asked my brother the other day what his overriding impression of our father was. I thought he would mention Dad's playfulness or his spirituality, but Jon thought awhile and replied, "Dad never lied to me, and he never broke a promise he had made. I trust him absolutely." That is the model that Elohim presents to us: Almighty Covenant God worthy of our faith and trust. And I hope that is our goal as we build a lifelong friendship with our sons. I hope when people are thinking of things to put on my tombstone that my son speaks up and says, "Put the words *faithful* and *honest* there, because he always kept his promises."

El Roi: the God Who Cares for Our Needs

A servant girl, alone, friendless, shamed, and afraid, crying in the wilderness to God, first introduces us to the fathering God who sees and cares. *El Roi* was the name Hagar called when she was fleeing Sarah's anger after conceiving a son by Abraham. Hagar had begun to lord it over Sarah that she was able to conceive when Sarah could not. Sarah became angry and mistreated Hagar, who fled from her anger and found herself in the wilderness alone, wondering no doubt how to provide and care for the baby she was carrying in her womb. El Roi responded by reaching down and touching her life with mercy. In response she called Him by that name, giving us insight into the character of our Father God.

The words describe for us a God who sees and cares. This is the fathering God who knows everything about His sons. He sees our fears and our failures. He feels our disappointments. He knows the sleepless nights. And He is there in the moment of inexpressible joy. El Roi sees our lives in intimate detail, and in seeing our lives He reaches into them with mercy, grace, and love. The good news for fathers is that the fathering God sees us. He understands the difficulty involved in fathering. He sees us struggle to keep our commitments. He feels our struggles to remain faithful to our promises. He watches us worry over our son's future and knows our hurt and grief when things go badly. He rejoices with us in times of happiness and sees the wondrous moments when we connect, maybe just for a flash of time, with our sons. He is the all-seeing Father; nothing escapes His vision. But instead of being an all-seeing God who wishes to punish us for our wrongdoing and our failures, this Father God, El Roi, wants to reach His hand out to us in compassion and love. El Roi sees and cares.

For fathers, El Roi is not only a source of comfort, He is also an inspiration. As fathers we would do well to model ourselves after the God who sees and cares. Often we do not take the time to look at and listen to our sons. We do not spend the time necessary to understand what is going on in their lives, and because of that we are unable to comfort or help them. Pay attention to your son as El Roi pays attention to you, and when you see him struggle, when you see him hurt, when you see him afraid and alone, reach out your hand, as the fathering God reaches out His hand, and bring a moment of grace and peace into your son's life.

It is awesome to really know your son, to be an attentive father. Being attentive allows us to hear our sons when they cry for help and to reach out and touch their lives. My son, Jonathon, was hiking in the mountains of Colorado with me awhile ago, and he wanted to climb up some rocks without me watching and worrying. He wanted to be on his own. So I walked a little ways away from him, turned behind a large boulder, and found a place where I could see Jonathon but he couldn't see me. I don't know how long I watched him play among the rocks, but it was a moment filled with wonder as I watched my son fearlessly leap from boulder to boulder. I hurried to keep up with him and scrambled to stay out of his sight while keeping him in my sight. All of a sudden I saw him falter. The rock was slippery, and Jonathon became afraid that he was going to fall. "Dad? Dad? Where are you? Help me, Dad," was his urgent cry. I stepped quickly from behind my hiding tree and reached my hand up to his. "You're OK, Jay. Just take my hand. I'll help you down." "You were watching me, Dad. Good! I was a little worried," he said with a sheepish grin as we scrambled back to our campsite together. Jonathon told the story to his mother about climbing from rock to rock. He omitted the part about being afraid and needing my help, but glanced my way when he came to that part of the story. I was glad in that moment that I had been a father who was watching, and in my watching was able to help.

You and I will have many more important opportunities to emulate El Roi than I did on that mountain. During your son's middle childhood years, he needs the seeing father who also protects. During your son's teenage years, he needs a father who sees and responds with compassion. No matter what their age, we need to see our sons, to know them, to stretch out our hands to them when they need help. El Roi is there for us and for our sons. As we try to father and they attempt to become men, El Roi gives us the quiet confidence that He sees us and will meet our needs. He cares.

Jehovah Ra-ah: the Shepherding Father

"I was lost, wandering around, trying to make it on my own, but God gathered me in and watched over me. He is my shepherd." So says a friend of mine who recently has found comfort and love through the tending of His shepherding Father in heaven. "The Lord is my shepherd, I shall not want" are the opening words to one of the best-known songs in the world. They are the words of the Psalmist David and introduce us to the 23rd Psalm. The phrase that is translated "The Lord is my Shepherd" comes from the Hebrew word *Jehovah Ra-ah*. The meaning is very simple: this is the shepherding God. He is the one who gathers His flock and keeps it safe and secure. He is the one who looks for the lost sheep. He is the Father God who tends to His flock, His children.

This image of God as shepherd always has comforted men and women. The fact that the God of the universe, with all of His power and glory, chooses to picture Himself as an all-seeing and all-caring shepherd tending His flock is almost too wondrous to believe. Think about it. This is the God who made the trees and set the stars in their places. He put the planets in motion and makes the rain fall and the sun shine. Yet He cares for us as a shepherd tends his flock.

What does that mean? It means that the fathering God watches over us carefully. Just as a shepherd's only task is to keep his flock safe from the predators that would steal them away and from the stupidity of their own actions, so the fathering God keeps His watch over us. And the image of God as the shepherding Father goes even further. This is the God who actively seeks out the wanderers in His flock. This Father chases after straying sheep, bringing them home safe in His arms. The message for us as fathers is clear. This God wants us in His flock. He wants us to give Him control over our families, and He promises to keep watch over them. He deeply loves His sheep. The image of God as shepherd also helps us see that no matter what we have done, no matter how we may have wronged our families, no matter how badly we feel we have blown it with our sons, the shepherding Father welcomes us back into His fold and promises rest in His care for our weary souls.

The lesson for own fathering we can take from Jehovah Ra-ah is clear. We are to be shepherds in our families. We are to keep watch over our sons when they are young and do our best to protect them and trust the shepherding Father to do the rest. We are to welcome straying teens back into the fold, and we are to never give up on our sons, just as the shepherding Father never gives up on a lost or wandering sheep. We also are responsible for our actions as shepherds of our little flock. That doesn't mean we are responsible for everything our children do wrong. Just as sheep are often victims of their own willfulness and ignorance, so our sons make their choices and must live with the consequences. As shepherds, our responsibility is to help set boundaries, to define for our sons where they may roam, and to welcome them back with open arms when they stray.

Jehovah-Shammah: the God Who Is Always There

"And the name of the city from that time on will be: THE LORD IS THERE." The Hebrew phrase *Jehovah-Shammah* (literally, "the Lord is present") ends the prophetic vision of the Book of Ezekiel (48:35). That promise has sustained generations of God's people as they put their faith in the Father God, who is there. The presence of the Lord was a reality in the lives of Abraham, Isaac,

Jacob, and Joseph that carried them through times of doubt and indecision. Jehovah-Shammah was with David when he wrote Psalm 139. Jehovah-Shammah was with Daniel in the lions' den. And Jehovah-Shammah is with us and our sons. This is the fathering God who doesn't leave us when things get difficult. Instead, He responds to adversity by standing and staying. This Father will not run away from His responsibilities or the ones He loves. He is Jehovah-Shammah; He is there and is not going anywhere.

In a day when fathers desert their children, leaving when things get tough, this kind of God stands out. Maybe your father walked out on you before you were born or during tough times when you were growing up. Maybe your father left you emotionally a long time ago and you feel the same stirrings in your heart. You wonder if you will be able to hang around for your son. You desperately want to avoid doing what your dad did, but the urge to run and hide has become almost unbearable.

Jehovah-Shammah's words to you are simple: "Take heart, I am the LORD your God and I am not going anywhere." The Father who is present always takes our woundedness as His own, understands the fears that drive us to run away physically or emotionally, and bids us stay with Him and learn from Him. What we learn from the Father who is present is that we don't have to run away when fathering gets tough. The Father God has watched His sons turn away and follow evil, but He always waits and hopes for their return. Even though Scripture speaks of God's heart being broken by the sinfulness of His children, still He is there, an unshakable presence. When your family becomes a difficult place to be, full of hurt and heartlessness instead of hope and love, Jehovah-Shammah has been there before and He is with you now. His words to us speak peace into our raging souls as He counsels us to be there for our sons, so that they can rest as easily as we can in the love of our Heavenly Father.

Our job as dads is to make our sons feel the reality of the God who is there. They need to sense our permanence in their lives. They need to know that even though divorce or distance may try to separate us, we will be there in every way we can for them. And even as we celebrate the grace of Jehovah-Shammah for His continued presence in our lives, so our children will get a glimpse of that God by watching us and knowing that we will be present in their lives.

Abba: the Fathering God

I was eight years old, walking home from school with my brother when it happened. Seven or eight kids from another school, much older than we were, jumped us as we passed a park a few blocks from our house. They held me down, hit me in the stomach, kicked me, threw my books and papers on the ground, and then ran away laughing as my brother and I lay on the ground and cried. We gathered up our stuff as best we could and ran home, fearful, sobbing, and looking everywhere for more bullies in the bushes. I ran straight over to my dad's office at church, threw my books down outside his door, burst into his study, and began to sob, "Daddy, Daddy, they, they beat me up, they took my stuff, they pounded on Jon. . . ." He just held me close and said, "You're with Daddy now. It's going to be OK."

In giving us the name *Abba*, God has let us do the same thing with Him that my father did with me. He has given us a personal way to call Him Father, to address Him as a lonely, hurt child addresses his dad. And then He holds us gently in His arms and says to us, "It's OK. Dad is here. You are safe." The words that Jesus used to describe His relationship to the fathering God reveal our relationship with the fathering God. Although He is Elohim and Jehovah in all of the power and glory those names suggest, He is also our Father. The word *Abba* is Aramaic and connotes a deep and abiding relationship. It shows us a fathering God who is approachable and dear to us. Hebrew children commonly used the name *Abba* to call their daddy, and children of God use it to call our Father. The name *Abba* is more than a diminutive though. It is not simply "daddy" in all of the familiarity that suggests. It also is used to convey the idea of a dear Father who cares and want His children to ask of Him. It tells us of a Father who desires our companionship and our love. It is almost awe-inspiring that the Creator of the universe has chosen to be known to us as Abba. It is almost beyond belief that the God who set the planets in motion and makes the skies rain wants us to call Him "Dear Father." This is the heart of our relationship as sons of the fathering God. He is not out there somewhere, unknowable and uncaring. He is the dear Father who wants the best for His children. He chooses to enter into a relationship with us that is intimate and powerful. He chooses to reveal Himself to us not only as Jehovah but as Dad. He invites us to be not merely servants but sons, members of the family. And He cares for us as a caring father loves his own sons.

The ultimate message of this fathering God is that He desires to be in relationship with us. He wants us to know Him, to love Him, to be part of His family. He invites all of us to become His sons, regardless of our background or social position. No matter what we have done before, there is a place in the family of God for all who respond to His invitation. He is Elohim, the God who keeps His promises. He is El Roi, the God who sees our needs and cares. He is Jehovah Ra-ah, the shepherding Father who gathers His flock. He is the ever-present Jehovah-Shammah, who will not leave us. And He is especially Abba, the fathering God who weeps when we weep, who holds us close and invites us into His family, into relationship with Him. He is the Father God, and we are His sons.

Chapter Fifteen

When All Is Said and Done

Don't take it all too seriously. Really, we mean it. *Fathers and Sons* is a serious book, and fathering sons, building a lifetime friendship with them, is a serious task, but don't take it all too seriously. Ultimately you and I cannot do everything in this book. The fathers and sons you have met in these pages don't do it all. They do some things well, and they work on the other things. If you walk away from reading this book and feel defeated or overwhelmed then we have failed, because we want *Fathers and Sons* to empower you, not send you off feeling that you don't measure up. We want *Fathers and Sons* to encourage you, not load you down with guilt.

What follows in this final chapter is our advice on how to put the fathering strengths to work in your life. Our prayer for you and your son is that this book will provide the impetus for you to begin to father intentionally, with a goal and a clear purpose in mind. We don't expect you to become "Father of the Year" overnight. But if you read these pages, feel compelled to make changes in your life, and then forget about it, we have failed in our purpose, and you will have settled for second best.

Assessment

The first step in putting the strengths found in this book to work in your fathering is to honestly assess how you are doing as a dad. Ask your wife what she thinks about the way you are fathering your son. Ask your own father. Ask your pastor. Ask your best friend. Ask them to honestly assess your fathering. Ask them if they notice any weaknesses that you need to work on, and then evaluate their answers. Don't dismiss them out of hand if they are negative, and don't assume they were just being nice to you if they give positive assessments. Find out what you can from others about your fathering. They have a perspective that is impossible for you to have, and hearing it will encourage and empower you.

The second step in assessment of your fathering is to use the self-tests and checklists in this book. If your son is a little bit older, ask for his help in filling out the checklists. Ask him for his input; ask him about your relationship. Use the tools in this book. They have been created especially for you, to help you build a stronger relationship with your son.

Thankfulness

After assessing your fathering and your relationship with your son, take a moment or two, or more if you are so inclined, to give the Father God thanks for the strengths in your relationship. If communication is a strength, be grateful and thank the Father God for helping you build that in your life. If you are doing an excellent job in handling conflict, be thankful for that. It is important that we don't focus only on what we are not doing, or what we are doing badly. Fathering sons can be difficult, and you need to stop and be thankful for the good things in your relationship.

Not long ago I was with a father and son who were having a difficult time in their relationship. The son had left for college and was seemingly turning his back on the values and beliefs of his father. The two of them argued constantly when the son was home and finally came to see me, to see what I could do to, in their words, "Straighten them out." I talked with them for a while and then asked this question to the son, "What do you like about your dad? What are your favorite things about him?" The son thought for a moment and then replied, "He has always been there for me, and I know that I can trust him no matter what." I turned to the father, "What do you like most about your son?" "I like his discipline, his work ethic, and I really admire his mind. He is a remarkable thinker, and I really admire that in him." "What do you like most about your relationship?" was the next question. The son replied first, "I like the fact that I can talk to Dad about anything and that he respects my opinion and listens to what I have to say." His father replied, "I like talking to him, hearing him think out loud, although lately I don't like what I'm hearing." He finished the sentence with a harrumph, and the softness that had come over his face was replaced with a frown.

"It seems to me that you guys are reaping the benefits of a strong relationship that is built on communication, but you don't see them as benefits," I told them. "The arguments you are having are possible because you trust and respect each other and because you talk so easily together, and now for the first time in your life you are disagreeing about something very important. But I have to tell you, I wish every family was like yours."

They looked at each other, smiled, looked at me with slightly puzzled grins, and began to argue again, but not with anger this time. Instead, they argued with conviction and a belief in the other person. Now, they will struggle occasionally, but seeing how truly strong their relationship was gave them the courage to exercise their strengths without fear of losing it. Once they saw how well they were doing, they became free to work on their relationship.

All of us need to see what we are doing right in our relationships with our sons. We need to hear what is good about our fathering, and we need to give thanks for the strengths that exist in our lives.

One Thing, for Starters

After figuring out what you are doing right in your relationship with your son, look at some of the strengths that are not present in your life, or ones that you want to build even more. Pick one thing to work on and then work on it. If you say to yourself, "I'm going to do all of these things, and I'm going to start right now!" you will fail because it is impossible to start every fathering strength

199

from nothing. One builds on another, and they grow slowly, with effort. Pick one thing you want to do well this year and then do it. Our advice is to work on time together or spiritual wellness. Those two give birth to most of the other strengths, and without those foundational strengths it is tough to do the others. But it is up to you. Pick a strength you want to work on, and follow the helps given in the book. If there is an activity in the book to help you get started, do it. And then follow through.

Don't Give Up

All of us father our sons badly at times. All of us go through times when we fail to be what we ought to be. That's OK. That's the price of being human, and there is forgiveness and there are second chances. Don't give up after a failure or after your son has rejected you. There is always hope and there is always tomorrow. Too many dads try for a few weeks or months, fail badly, and then never again try to become the fathers to their sons that they could be. Don't do that. Hang with it and don't give up.

When All Is Said and Done

Most of all realize that doing your best is all that you can do, and that when all is said and done, your best is enough. There is no such animal as a perfect relationship. Every father and son experience peaks and valleys in their relationship. Every father and son have moments of closeness followed by days or weeks of distance. That's OK; that is normal. We don't want to create an unrealistic expectation for you. Your relationship will never be "just perfect." There is always something to work on, another area to grow. It is unrealistic to expect to always be close to each other. It is unrealistic to expect completely open communication all of the time. It is unrealistic to expect to deal with conflict perfectly every time it arises. It is not fair or realistic to expect your son to respond to every overture you make to him.

But many fathers aren't even trying, and that is a mistake. A strong friendship with your son, realistic and honest in its expectations, can be one of the most fulfilling relationships in your life. It is a big deal, and it deserves to be our goal. But to echo the opening words of this chapter, don't take it all too seriously. Don't approach your relationship with your son with a "nose to the grindstone attitude." Approach it with a sense of wonder and joy, hoping for the best, understanding the limitations of human relationships, and trusting God to work in your life and in the life of your son.

My father and I fight too much. We spend too much time together, and often we are cranky with each other. Sometimes Dad expects too much of me; sometimes I expect too little of myself. Sometimes we both make mistakes that end up hurting each other; sometimes we take our relationship for granted. But most of the time my friendship with my dad is one of the most satisfying and enriching things in my life. It draws me to God with thankfulness for His grace on our friendship, and I am constantly aware of how much work Dad has put into our life together. Most of the time my friendship with my father is a source of joy and laughter, and in many ways he is my best friend.

I love my dad and he loves me. And together we are committed to making our friendship last until one of us passes from this place; and then the one left behind will still have the comfort of thousands of memories and a love that lingers far beyond death's door, and the anticipation of a reunion, when we all meet the fathering God in His house together.

That is our prayer for you and your son.

2424